POLLING
Statistical Case Studies for Political and Public Affairs Research

Michael D. Lieberman

243 West 99th Street
New York, NY 10025
IBN 979-8-30-432369-7

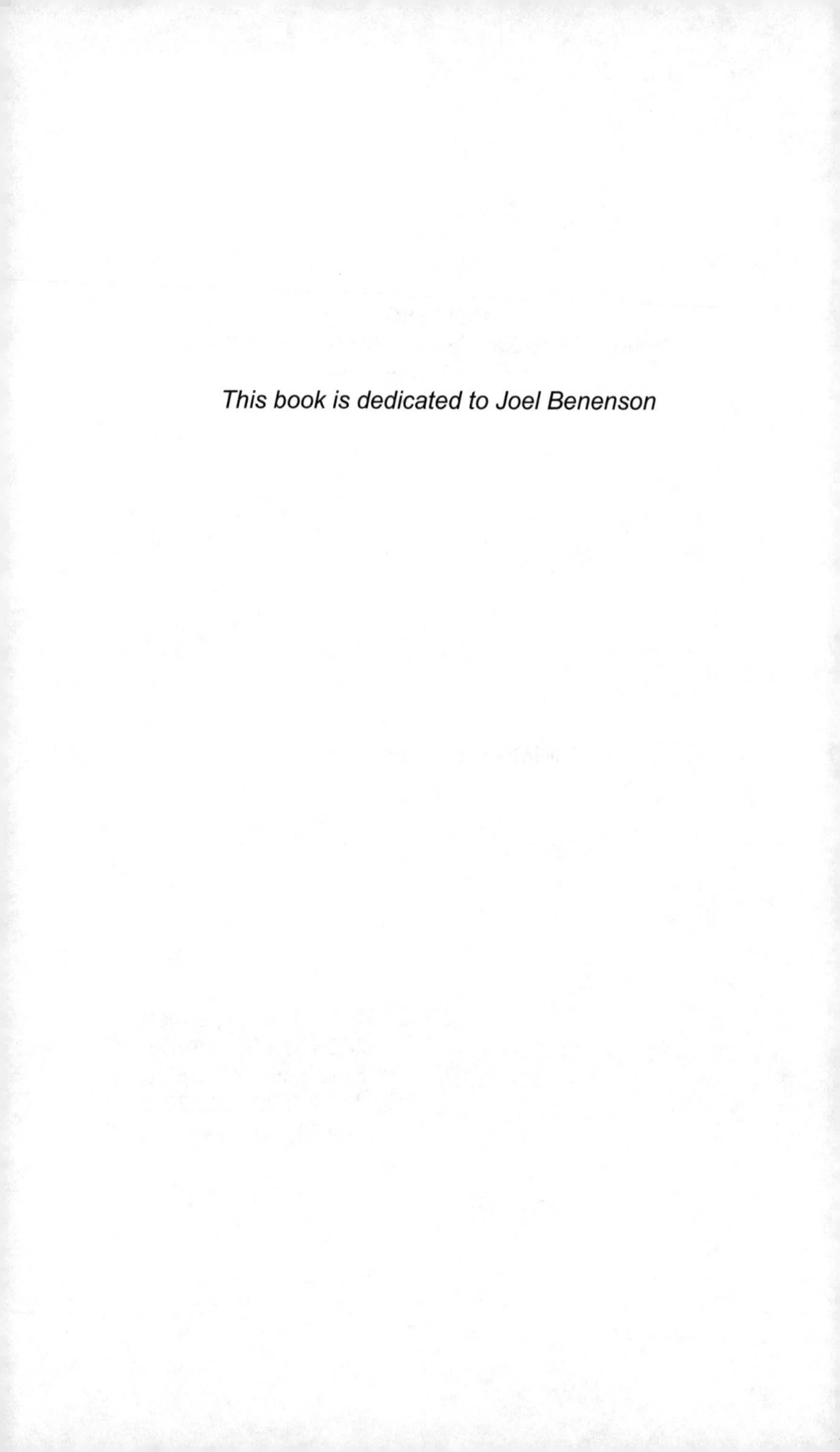

This book is dedicated to Joel Benenson

Contents

Kickoff to Political Polling - Beginning the Research Process

Multivariate political polling involves analyzing multiple variables simultaneously to understand complex relationships between political opinions and various demographic, psychological, or contextual factors. This approach helps researchers identify patterns, interactions, and correlations that might not be evident through simpler, univariate or bivariate analysis. The research process begins with defining clear objectives, focusing on questions like how different factors (e.g., age, education, political affiliation) influence voter preferences or policy opinions.

Once objectives are established, survey design is the next critical step. Researchers must develop questions that capture the nuances of multiple variables. For instance, a question about candidate preference might be paired with questions on socio-economic status, education level, and media consumption habits. The structure of the survey must account for these variables without overwhelming respondents or introducing bias.

Initial research objectives in political polling aim to define the purpose and scope of the study. Key objectives include identifying voter preferences, understanding public opinion on specific policies, and assessing candidate approval ratings.

Researchers may also explore demographic influences on political behaviors, such as age, education, or income levels, and how these factors correlate with voter turnout or issue-based support. These objectives guide the survey design, sampling methods, and data analysis, ensuring that the research provides valuable insights for political campaigns, media coverage, or policy-making decisions. Figure 1 outlines the agenda of an initial meeting for the research and campaign strategy teams.

Figure 1 – Initial Research Objectives

INITIAL RESEARCH OBJECTIVES

- **Who** lives in your district;
- **How Many** votes does the candidate need to **win**;
- **Which** issues are important to them and what they think about these Key Issues;
- **What** they think about you and your rival, and why;
- **How** to use your critical resources – time, money, staff and volunteers – most effectively.

A successful campaign is much like a thriving business—it must understand its audience and strategically deploy resources to gain a competitive edge. Just as businesses rely on accurate data to optimize their assets, campaigns need precise information to effectively target their efforts and maximize impact.

Campaign research starts with a baseline survey, collecting insights via phone, online, or in-person interviews from a scientifically chosen sample. This process evaluates the political landscape, voter demographics, party affiliations, and both positive and negative perceptions of the candidates. These insights form the foundation for shaping campaign strategies.

Polling data must then be thoroughly analyzed to guide clear, effective, and actionable strategic decisions.

Inputs into a campaign communication strategy include a comprehensive understanding of voter demographics, polling data, issue priorities, and public perception of the candidate and opponents. This strategy is shaped by identifying the core messages that resonate with key voter groups, analyzing the media landscape, and understanding the platforms where target audiences are most active.

Figure 2 – Inputs into Campaign Communication Strategy

These techniques allow researchers to analyze multiple variables simultaneously, uncovering complex relationships and patterns that may be missed with simpler methods.

We cover widely used methods such as multiple regression, factor analysis, cluster analysis, and principal component analysis. Each chapter provides a step-by-step guide to applying these techniques, supported by real-world examples and case studies. By the end, readers will have a solid understanding of how to use multivariate analysis to draw meaningful insights from their data.

Political Branding – Setting the Table and Candidate Image

Political branding refers to the strategic creation and management of a political entity's image to influence public perception and garner support. It involves crafting a clear identity that conveys values, vision, and policies, much like corporate branding. Political parties, candidates, and movements use branding to differentiate themselves from competitors and connect emotionally with voters. Key elements include slogans, logos, messaging, and media presence.

Successful political branding helps establish trust, loyalty, and recognition, making it easier for candidates or parties to communicate their platforms. Ultimately, it aims to build a lasting, favorable impression in the minds of constituents.

When most people think about a brand's identity, they usually think about the name, logo, or perhaps its advertising jingle (*It's the Real Thing*). Identity, however, is a far more complex myriad of association that might include package design, brand voice, attitudes, and brand personality (product utility, visual style, etc.) The list could go on.

The most powerful brands maintain a consistent voice and visual style, which serve as valuable assets when expanding into new markets or launching new products. This brand consistency builds trust and recognition among consumers, allowing brands to leverage their established reputation as they introduce new offerings.

The same applies to a political brand. Consistent messaging and design reinforce a campaign's identity, making it more recognizable and trustworthy. This strategic use of message equity not only strengthens voter loyalty but also facilitates success when expanding into new constituencies or launching statewide or national campaigns. By maintaining coherence, political brands create a sense of familiarity and credibility, which is essential for building support and winning over broader audiences. This consistency helps ensure that the brand resonates across various regions and voter demographics, enhancing its overall impact.

For example, political brand extensions are the 'story' told to sell the campaign. In 1960, John F. Kennedy's 'New Frontier'. For Ronald Reagan in 1984, it was 'Morning in America. Barak Obama's campaign emphasized hope, change, and unity, with a focus on reforming healthcare, the economy, and foreign policy. His message, 'Yes we can.' For Donald Trump, 'Make America Great Again.'

Political branding can profoundly impact the American political landscape. Gingrich's "Contract with America" ignited a conservative revolution, uniting fiscal and social conservatives under a cohesive vision. This branding positioned the Republican Party as the defender of fiscal responsibility, moral values, limited government, and national security—claims not fully realized in practice. However, it demonstrates branding's power: when effectively communicated, it can overshadow reality, offering comfort and trust to those who believe in its message. The Republican Party's success in building this image shows how a well-crafted narrative can shape public perception, even when it diverges from actual achievements.

Measuring The Message

According to a well-known axiom, you can't manage what you can't measure. This is true of the message as well. Message measurement should measure:

- Campaign awareness (first mention, unaided awareness, top-of-mind, and total recall)
- Campaign preference
- Issue importance/rank in consideration set
- Issue relevance

- Emotional connection
- Loyalty (what are the loyalists saying that is consistent with the undecideds?)
- Campaign Imagery

For example, there's an open congressional seat in a local race—the type of opportunity ambitious lower-level politicians eagerly pursue. Liz Anderson, a local attorney and state senator wants a promotion and decides to enter the race, preparing for what will likely be a crowded primary. Our team is brought in to conduct an initial poll to evaluate her chances and help craft her campaign message.

Sections of the Initial Questionnaire
We want to distinguish him from his many primary opponents. Below are what I would deem the most important aspects to measure:

- Unaided candidate awareness, particularly first recall
- Candidate experience
- Knowledge of campaign potential (what does the average voter have to gain by supporting this candidate)
- The perception of delivery against key campaign promises (all candidates promise their mother during the race. What is important is that they are not *perceived* to be promising their mother, when they have no intention of handing her over).
- Accessibility
- Emotional connection (otherwise known as brand personality)

Figure 1 – Top-of-Mind vs. Aided Candidate Awareness

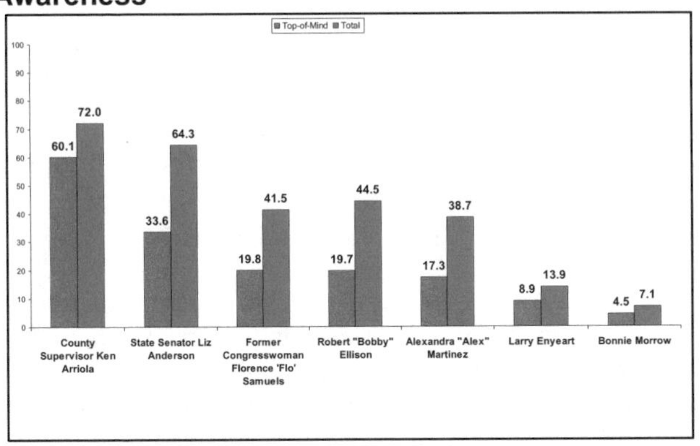

In fact, incorporating all these elements into an initial poll is quite simple. The survey is concise. For instance, regarding candidate experience, include an open-ended question for respondents familiar with the candidate. Campaign potential and perceived effectiveness can be evaluated through a brief list of attributes that either describe or rate the candidate. Emotional connection can be gauged by asking respondents to rank the importance of local issues, reflecting how well the candidate resonates with voters.

Ask those who are aware of the candidate how likely they are to vote for Liz Anderson. They run a simple regression analysis to assess her brand 'equity'. That is, those issues or attributes that pop out of the regressions are the why those folks are supporting Liz Anderson. Her brand equity, and perhaps the basis of her campaign strategy and the shaping of her message.

Message Marketing

Although campaign management and advertising are two of the more important and visible components of the race, it is agreed that message management is much more holistic and interdependent than that. Campaign discipline, relaying the message, is tantamount.

Effective message integration should have the following aspects:

Create a well-communicated campaign position statement that includes the target audience, the campaign essence, promise, and personality.

Create a kitchen cabinet, that close circle of friends and advisors the candidate needs to surround him. The kitchen cabinet are those who can tell the candidate what he might not want to hear, what might be difficult for 'staff' to bring up.

Conduct campaign communications workshops with the 'kitchen cabinet'.

Appoint a Message Visionary Early: As election day approaches, campaigns often get bogged down in daily operations. Ensure there is a dedicated strategist at the top who prioritizes messaging. This person should determine what reaches the candidate each day so that when they board the campaign train, conduct radio interviews, or engage with voters, they stay consistently on message.

Define Clear Message Objectives: Messaging should be driven by polling insights and strategic goals. Establish a clear plan to shift undecided voters into the probably category. Effective research will identify the most efficient way to achieve this.
Create message, program, and segment plans. What speaks to the African-American Protestant ministers might not sway, say, working soccer moms.

Develop integrated media plans.

Political branding plays a crucial role in shaping candidate image and setting the stage for successful campaigns. A well-crafted brand strategy allows candidates to communicate their values, vision, and strengths effectively to voters, creating an emotional connection and fostering loyalty. By maintaining consistency in messaging and visuals, political campaigns can establish credibility and differentiate themselves in a competitive landscape. Ultimately, a strong political brand not only enhances voter perception but also builds a foundation for long-term success, ensuring that candidates resonate with the electorate and leave a lasting impact on the political scene.

Likely Voters Models: The Key to Accurate Electoral Analysis

In the fiercely contested 2024 election, 245 million Americans were registered to vote. However, as reported by *U.S. News & World Report*, about 90 million of them—roughly 37%—did not cast a ballot. This underscores a critical limitation of polls based on registered voters: they inherently include a substantial margin of error, making it nearly impossible to achieve an electoral forecast with a ±3% margin of accuracy.

In close elections like 2024, this discrepancy can create the impression that the polls were "wrong." Yet, as *ABC News* noted, “the average poll conducted during the final three weeks of the campaign missed the election margin by just 2.94 percentage points.”

The *average* poll had a 3% margin of error, meaning some polls performed better, offering greater predictive accuracy. These more reliable polls are typically based on ‘likely voters’ rather than simply ‘registered voters,’.

Polling error differs between samples of likely voters and registered voters due to variations in voter turnout assumptions, modeling techniques, and the composition of the sample. The average polling error for likely voter samples is typically around 2-3%. In contrast, surveys based on registered voters generally exhibit higher error rates, at least one percentage point greater, typically around 4-5%—as this group includes individuals who are less likely to vote.

Here we explore the most commonly used likely voter models, detailing how they identify individuals most likely to participate in an election. It examines methodologies such as self-reported voting intentions, past voting behavior, and demographic indicators. By analyzing these approaches, the chapter highlights their strengths, limitations, and effectiveness in enhancing polling accuracy.

Background

All major polling firms employ likely voter models. These models integrate demographic data, past voting behavior, and survey responses. Approaches vary, from simple self-reported likelihood to sophisticated algorithms. Accurate likely voter models are critical for reliable polling results.

The most famous likely voter model, developed more than a half century ago by Gallup in use today by the Pew Research Center, estimates voter turnout through survey questions on voting likelihood, past behavior, interest, and knowledge. Responses are scored and weighted based on demographics such as age, education, and race. Calibrated to turnout trends, this model effectively identifies likely voters and predicts election outcomes.

Figure 1 - Pew Research Center's American Trends Panel Weighting Dimensions

American Trends Panel weighting dimensions

Variable	Benchmark source
Age (detailed) Age x Gender Education x Gender Education x Age Race/Ethnicity x Education Race/Ethnicity x Gender Black (alone or in combination) x Hispanic Born inside vs. outside the U.S. among Hispanics and Asian Americans Years lived in the U.S. Census region x Metropolitan status	2022 American Community Survey (ACS)
Volunteerism	2021 CPS Volunteering & Civic Life Supplement
Voter registration	2020 CPS Voting and Registration Supplement
Frequency of internet use Religious affiliation Party affiliation x Race/Ethnicity Party affiliation among registered voters	2024 National Public Opinion Reference Survey (NPORS)

Note: Estimates from the ACS are based on noninstitutionalized adults. Voter registration is calculated using procedures from Hur, Achen (2013) and rescaled to include the total U.S. adult population.

PEW RESEARCH CENTER

No likely voter model remains consistently the most accurate. Much like a hedge fund manager who initially outperforms market indices but eventually regresses to the mean, the effectiveness of a likely voter model fluctuates depending on the election, demographic trends, and data quality. While a model may excel at predicting turnout in certain elections, it can also misjudge key groups or levels of voter enthusiasm. No single model maintains top accuracy across multiple election cycles.

Building a Likely Voter Model Survey

A likely voter model predicts voter turnout by incorporating key elements: voter registration status, past voting behavior, demographics (age, income, education), political interest, partisanship, poll responses, early voting history, state turnout trends, election-specific factors (e.g., competitiveness), and survey weighting techniques to estimate actual turnout probabilities accurately.

Below are the key elements of an effective likely voter model survey. Within this framework, political statisticians can evaluate the most effective model for a given electoral cycle.

Figure 2 - Elements of a Likely Voter Model Questionnaire

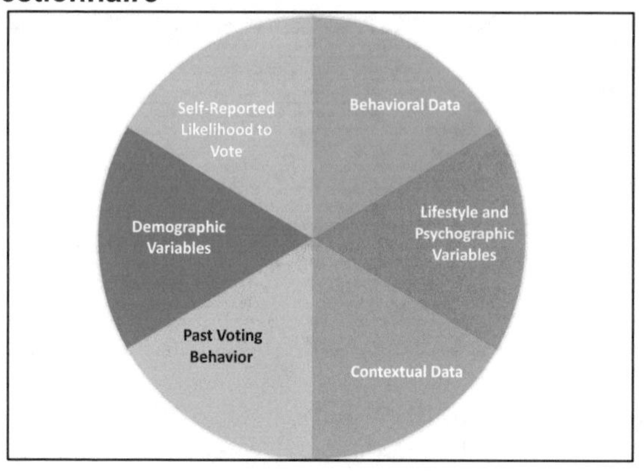

Derived metrics play a crucial role in the process as well. For instance, a turnout propensity score provides a numerical prediction of an individual's likelihood to vote based on model inputs. Vote history matches past voting records with survey data, enabling a more comprehensive analysis. Additionally, demographic weighting adjusts the model to account for population or sample demographics, ensuring greater accuracy and representativeness.

Popular Predictive Models for Estimating Likely Voter Turnout

Likely Voter Models utilize predictive analytics to estimate voter turnout by analyzing historical data through statistical algorithms and machine learning. Predictive models often integrate tools like voter turnout scores or microtargeting strategies. With advancements in computing power and open-source tools like the R programming languages, the new power of Excel, or the ubiquitous SPSS, a few lines of code can now streamline data processing, focusing efforts only on those most likely to vote.

Table 1 – Most Common Predictive Models for Likely Voters

Model	Primary Usage
Logistic Regression	Predicting a binary outcome, such as whether an individual will vote or not.
Decision Trees	Segmenting voters into groups based on their likelihood of voting.
Random Forests	Combining multiple decision trees to improve accuracy.
Neural Networks	Modeling complex patterns and interactions in data. Suitable for large datasets with many features. Neural networks also capture non-linear relationships effectively.
k-Nearest Neighbors (k-NN)	Classifying individuals based on the behavior of similar individuals.
Naïve Bayes	Estimating probabilities of voter turnout based on Bayes' theorem (Bayes' Theorem is a mathematical formula used to calculate the *probability* of voting likelihood based on prior knowledge and new evidence).
Ensemble Models	Combining multiple models (e.g., bagging, boosting) for better performance. One R statistical module, Caret, includes over 240 models that can be used for classification, regression, and other types of analyses.
Time Series Models	Predicting turnout trends based on temporal data--refers to data that is associated with time or has a time-related dimension and captures how something changes or evolves over time.

Global Applications of Likelihood Voting Models

International case studies showcase the adaptability and versatility of likelihood voting models in diverse political settings. These examples illustrate how such models are tailored to different electoral systems, utilizing local data inputs like demographics, voter turnout trends, and socioeconomic factors. By doing so, likelihood voting models effectively inform voter mobilization efforts and campaign strategies on a global scale. Table 2 (below) highlights some of the most notable applications from the past decade.

Table 2 – International Case Studies of Predictive Likelihood Voters Models

Election	Model Used	Application
Obama's 2008 and 2012 Campaigns (United States)	Logistic Regression, Random Forests	Identified undecided and infrequent voters to target with tailored GOTV (Get Out The Vote) efforts.
Trump's 2016 Campaign (United States)	Decision Trees, Psychographic Profiling	Microtargeted persuadable voters in key battleground states using behavioral and demographic data.
Brexit Referendum (United Kingdom, 2016)	Gradient Boosting Machines (GBMs)	Predicted turnout trends to focus campaign efforts in regions with high undecided voters.
Macron's 2017 Presidential Campaign (France)	Random Forests, Logistic Regression	Modeled likely voter turnout to prioritize campaign resources.
Indian General Election (2024)	Neural Networks, Decision Trees	Used social media and smartphone penetration data to predict voter preferences and turnout.
Australian Federal Election (2019)	Random Forests, Naïve Bayes	Predicted preferences under the ranked-choice voting system.
Colombian Peace Referendum (2016)	Logistic Regression	Identified regional turnout
South African Local Elections (2021)	Decision Trees, Gradient Boosting	Predicted turnout in urban and peri-urban areas using socioeconomic and political trust data.
Kenyan Presidential Election (2022)	Support Vector Machines (SVM), Time Series	Models Predicted turnout and vote shares based on demographic and geographic data.
European Union Elections (2014)	Logistic Regression, Ensemble Models	Predicted turnout trends in countries with historically low participation.
Israeli Elections (2022)	Logistic Regression, Neural Networks	Modeled voter turnout to counteract political apathy in younger demographics
German Federal Elections (2021)	Ensemble Models, Time Series	Modeled turnout and sentiment to predict shifts in party support.
Chilean Constitutional Referendum (2020)	Logistic Regression	Predicted voter turnout in urban centers where constitutional change was contentious.
Scottish Independence Referendum (2014)	Decision Trees, Time Series Models	Predicted turnout patterns in favor of "Yes" and "No" campaigns based on geographic and demographic data.

Identifying likely voters is a critical component of accurate political research and election forecasting. As this chapter has demonstrated, the mathematical models used to predict voter turnout are invaluable tools, but they are not infallible. While self-reported intentions, past behavior, and demographic indicators provide powerful insights, their effectiveness hinges on the context of the election, the quality of data, and the evolving dynamics of the electorate.

No single model works universally; each has strengths and limitations that researchers must weigh carefully. The key to improving accuracy lies in adapting methodologies to new trends, refining assumptions, and acknowledging the inherent uncertainties in human behavior. Ultimately, the pursuit of the "perfect" likely voter model may be elusive, but the iterative process of refinement and innovation ensures that these tools remain indispensable in the ever-changing landscape of political research.

Strategic Regression - What Is Driving The Vote
The campaign is beginning. The message is being formed. Surveys are conducted with the challenge to find the *winner*—the message that will carry your guy into office and the other guy into the retirement home. What you emphasize, where you defend your ground, and how to attack.

The challenge is to produce the results within either the context of existing research, or within a short, budget friendly snapshot poll that can reproduced easily to track progress and keep costs down.

Regression models use linear equations across multiple factors—such as issue importance, message acceptance, and statement agreement ratings—to determine which issues have the greatest impact on voter preference. Strategic regression analysis delivers clear, actionable insights that are both easy to understand and effectively communicate.

Regression 101
Strategic regression analysis measures the *strength* of descriptive attributes or performance ratings *in relation to* a strategic characteristic. The strategic characteristic is 'Will vote your candidate.' 'Will vote for the other guy,' or 'Level of support for this initiative', 'Overall performance rating of the government.' A critical issue that the campaign wishes to understand and affect.

The first step, after asking the respondent about their voting preference, is to create a list of key issues, policies, or support statements that can shape the campaign's message. For example, using a 1-to-7 scale, respondents are asked to rate how important various topics are to them personally, such as "Ensuring access to affordable healthcare for everyone" or "A woman's right to choose abortion." These topics, relevant to the campaign, help build a coherent message or platform once they are gathered and analyzed.

The format of issue statements can vary from a traditional scale. For instance, to determine whether a respondent associates a statement more with either all candidates, you might ask about traits like "Honest" or "Effective—gets things done."

When measuring support for a specific initiative, such as building a new trash compactor, the statements might look like, "How strongly do you agree with the following: 'The new incinerator would prevent toxins from leaching into the ground,'" or "'The new incinerator is projected to last 100 years, whereas the current one may fail within 10.'" These statements are then analyzed alongside a general support question for the initiative, revealing the key factors driving people's backing of the project.

The strength of this technique lies in its ability to be filtered by key voting demographics without extending the survey. It can be segmented by factors like gender, race, or age, or by more specific voter groups—such as men over 50 who live in suburban areas, earn over $100,000, and play golf three times a week. These groups can be combined in various ways, and the analysis will reveal the key drivers for each. Applying filters in this way generates a much richer set of insights compared to traditional tabulation methods.

Conducting Regression Analysis

Linear regression analysis leverages the ratings of independent variables along with the corresponding ratings of the dependent variable to create a linear equation that predicts the dependent variable. This equation produces beta coefficients, which are then multiplied by the independent variables after the equation is determined.

In other words, the beta gives the *weight* of the issue or statement in predicting who the respondent is going to vote for.

There are two short next steps and the interpretation begins.

The first is to rank the issues by their beta weights. This gives the order of importance for the issues in relation to vote preference.

The next step is to identify the beta coefficients that are statistically significant. Essentially, each regression equation assumes that the beta scores are equal to zero, meaning they have no impact. However, we are focused on the issues that do have an impact—those that are significant. In presentations, we emphasize only the significant issues to demonstrate their influence, while ignoring those that are not. Typically, I set the threshold at 90%, meaning I aim to be at least 90% confident that the issue affects voter preference or support.

Within a political context significance can be either positive or negative. Positive issues drive the vote up. As they rise, so does voting percentage.

Negative significance drives the votes down. As they rise, the vote drops. For example, in a poll 'Abortion rights' was negatively significant for Candidate A. What that translates into is that those people who are for abortion rights are against Candidate A. A good piece of information for Candidate B.

Tactics for Leveraging Campaign Regression Outcomes
There are three ways to use the information. 1) Promote, 2) Defend your ground, and 3) Attack your opponent.

Your Candidate: Positive Significance - Promote those issues or qualities that are positive and significant for your candidate. Our research shows 'Loves Dogs' is driving the vote for Democratic candidate Jonathan Reed. Tell the public, 'Jonathan Reed Loves Dogs'. Run on the issues that are of high importance to those who plan to vote for you.

Your Candidate: Negative Significance - Defend your position is crucial when an issue appeals to supporters of both candidates. For instance, if research shows that "Loves Dogs" is a key driver not only for Jonathan Reed but also for his opponent, Republican Amanda Collins, Jonathan Reed cannot afford to relinquish this ground. While "Loves Dogs" may not be the defining issue of the race, Jonathan Reed needs to maintain his stance on it.

Have Jonathan Reed's speechwriter include a line like, "My opponent claims we don't care about dogs. The truth is, we love dogs and are doing more for them than our opponent, who has never even owned one."

Opposition: Positive Or Negative Significance - Critique Their Strengths While Emphasizing Their Weaknesses. Strategic regression tells your campaign to either attack your opponent's positives or promote his negatives. Returning to an earlier example, 'Abortion rights' is a negative driver for Jonathan Reed. Amanda Collins should be pushing his dubious opinion on the freedom of choice. As this becomes known, the research indicates that support for him will drop.

Similarly, if "Supporting the Trash Compactor" is a positive driver for your opponent, challenge his support as insincere or criticize the initiative as a mere gimmick. If public confidence in your opponent's sincerity or the initiative declines, so will support for him, as his campaign is built around this issue.

A Sample Campaign

It is August, the dog days of summer, time of squeezing hands during beach (if there is a beach in your state) barbecues and back-to-school sales. Also time to prepare the message for the campaign, which begins in earnest after Labor Day. A poll is being conducted to determine your candidate's name position, that of your opponent, and the winning message you wish to bring to the effort.

In the survey, respondents were initially asked who they would vote for. Afterward, they were presented with a list of key issues and asked to determine whether each issue was more relevant to Jonathan Reed or Amanda Collins. The issues are outlined below.

Issue importance ratings are listed below:

- Abortion Rights
- Gun Control
- Climate Change and Environmental Policy
- Foreign Policy and National Security
- Economy and Inflation
- Immigration Reform
- Racial Justice and Policing Reform
- Healthcare Reform
- Education and Curriculum
- Fiscal Integrity

Respondents were then asked about which personal qualities applied more to the two candidates. These personal qualities are summarized here:

- Integrity—A good politician is honest, transparent, and upholds strong moral principles.

- Communication Skills—Effective communication, both in public speaking and listening.
- Decision-Making Ability—A good politician can make informed, thoughtful decisions.
- Leadership—Strong leadership inspires confidence, mobilizes people toward common goals.
- Vision—A good politician has a clear, long-term vision for the future.
- Hard Working—A good politician works hard for the people.
- Honesty— A good politician is honest and transparent with their constituents.
- Adaptability—The ability to adjust strategies, policies, and approaches based on changing circumstances.
- Accountability—A responsible politician is willing to be held accountable for their actions and decisions, admitting mistakes and working to correct them.
- Diplomacy—The ability to engage in negotiations, manage conflicts, and build consensus among diverse groups.

Among the two key groups the following issues and qualities came up significant for the two candidates.

Table 1 -Summarization Key Drivers for Jonanthan Reed and Amanda Collins

Candidate	Positive Significant Drivers	Negative Significant Drivers
Jonathan Reed		
Issues	Climate Change and Environmental Policy	Economy and Inflation
	Abortion Rights	Immigration Reform
Qualities	Effective	Vision
	Hard-Working	
Amanda Collins		
Issues	Fiscal Integrity	Gun Control
	Immigration Reform	
Qualities	Strong Leadership Skills	Diplomacy
	Communication Skills	Honesty

From the analysis the strategy emerges. Jonathan Reed is running on a platform where he is a leading advocate of climate chance and a woman's right to choose. He is seen as effective and hard-working.

The Jonathan Reed campaign must also address his weaknesses. He is not seen as fiscally astute, and his progressive stance on immigration may be viewed as too far left for his constituents. These are challenges that need attention.

Jonathan Reed's opponent, Amanda Collins, is seen as fiscally responsible and is more hardline on immigration. Key drivers for her voters are that she is seen as a strong person with very good communication skills.

Amanda Collins has her own weaknesses. She is perceived as being influenced by the NRA, lacks diplomacy, and is not widely seen as honest.

Whether you work for the Jonathan Reed or Amanda Collins media teams, a roadmap is provided outlining key points to emphasize in campaign communications and strategy.

Visualizing Regression Analysis

Visualizing regression analysis makes it easier for clients to understand complex statistical relationships by turning abstract data into intuitive visuals. Graphs, scatter plots, and trend lines help demonstrate how variables are related and provide a clear picture of predicted outcomes versus actual results.

Clients can see how well the model fits the data, identify trends, and spot outliers. This visual representation makes it simpler to explain the impact of different variables, making the information more digestible than numbers alone. It also helps in communicating the reliability and accuracy of predictions, fostering better decision-making and trust in the analysis.

Visualizing regression output using flowcharts can be an effective way to simplify the decision-making process involved in regression analysis. Flowcharts break down the sequence of steps, making it easier to understand how the model was built and how predictions are made. Here's how it works:

- Start the flowchart with boxes representing independent variables (predictors).
- Model Output: Highlight the regression equation or coefficients as a result of the training.
- Prediction: Lead to the final box representing predicted values or outcomes, with possible decision paths based on the predictions.

Table 2 – Flow Chart Visual – Regression Analysis

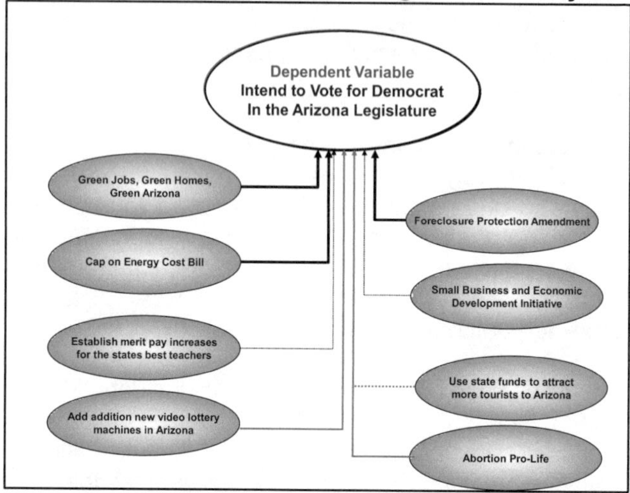

Strategic regression analysis is one of several statistical techniques that enhances the value of existing polls and providing strategists with crucial insights for planning.

In the context of a rapidly evolving campaign, where candidates seek more information and cost-effective solutions, strategic regression analysis provides clear, actionable insights that clients can understand and apply immediately.

Tiered Regression - Steering the Vote: The Case of Oglala Sioux Casino

The United States is deeply divided along political lines, with significant differences in how various issues are perceived by members of the two major parties, Democrats and Republicans. Democrats tend to prioritize issues such as climate change, social justice, and healthcare reform, advocating for more government intervention to address systemic inequalities and environmental concerns.

On the other hand, Republicans often focus on issues like economic deregulation, individual liberties, and national security, favoring limited government involvement and a strong emphasis on traditional values. These ideological differences are reflected in starkly contrasting views on policies related to immigration, gun control, and healthcare, leading to a polarized political landscape where consensus is increasingly difficult to achieve.

Based on my experience in conducting political surveys, it's clear that the issues that mobilize one group of voters often differ from those that resonate with another. Most elections, referendums, or voter measures are driven by two distinct sets of priorities, with each side motivated by different concerns and factors.

Tiered regression consists of two steps. The first step—the initial regression—is driving the underlying sales pitch of a campaign: what a candidate stands for, what a new referendum will accomplish, or the basic reasoning behind a measure.

The second 'layer' of regression involves attributes that can *sway* voters' opinions in either direction. Sway, in this instance, is defined by improving voters views on a single issue, be that from strongly oppose to neutral, neutral to support, and support to strongly support.

Tiered regression uses a widely utilized survey design that can pinpoint both types of drivers. The survey we use is no longer than a typical one (since time is money in the field), but by carefully structuring the questions, we can capture both the initial appeal and the factors that sway voters—essentially doubling the insights—without extending the survey's length.

The Oglala Sioux of Rapid City
In South Dakota, tensions have arisen between Native American tribes operating casinos and some white residents, particularly in rural areas. The tribes view casinos as a crucial source of revenue that supports tribal sovereignty, funds essential services, and creates jobs within their communities.

However, some white residents have expressed concerns about the social and economic impacts of these casinos, including increased competition for local businesses, changes in community dynamics, and moral objections to gambling. These tensions are further complicated by historical grievances, land disputes, and the broader economic disparities between Native American tribes and non-Native communities, leading to ongoing debates over the role and regulation of tribal casinos in the state.

The Oglala Sioux Reservation is located near the Black Hills, home to popular tourist sites like Mount Rushmore, as well as the Rapid City metropolitan area. Rapid City is the second-largest city in South Dakota, with a population of around 70,000, approximately 75% of whom are classified as 'white alone,' a group we'll refer to as "Anglo." Unlike many other cities, Rapid City has a low percentage of 'traditional' minority groups, such as Black, Hispanic, or Asian populations. Instead, its largest minority group is Native American, at about 12% of residents.

Small cities in the U.S. Upper Midwest face a variety of social problems, often linked to economic shifts and rural isolation. The decline of traditional industries such as manufacturing and agriculture has led to job losses, stagnant wages, and reduced economic mobility, contributing to higher levels of poverty and financial insecurity. This region also grapples with significant public health issues, including the opioid epidemic and rising rates of alcohol and substance abuse.

To compound these ills, tensions between the White and Native populations are exacerbated by inequality. The Native American community, which represents a significant portion of the city's population, often experiences disproportionate levels of poverty, unemployment, and lack of access to healthcare and education compared to the white population. Racial tensions between Native Americans and the Anglo population have been longstanding, with incidents of discrimination and marginalization further straining relations.

To alleviate high unemployment and other long-standing social issues, the Oglala Sioux people of Pennington County, South Dakota, have proposed opening a gaming facility. However, they must secure the backing of a majority of white voters for the measure to pass.

An earlier poll indicated these specific reasons for opposing the new gaming permit:

- This measure will lead to an increase in gambling addictions, bankruptcies and other social problems;
- Passage of this measure could lead to major expansion of gambling in the state;

As earlier poll revealed a systemic, though subtle, prejudice within the Anglo community against the Oglala Sioux, along with a clear concern that gaming would attract the 'wrong elements' to the Black Hills and

Rapid City. Native Americans, including the Oglala Sioux and other tribes such as the Lakota and mainstream Sioux, who are likely to support the referendum, account for only 10% of registered voters. As a result, a significant number of non-Native voters would need to be persuaded for the referendum to succeed.

As the saying goes, "If you don't like what people are saying, change the conversation." Our firm was engaged to identify the most effective talking points. The Oglala Sioux council, along with their public relations team, sought to understand why voters supported or opposed the measure and which elements of the referendum they should highlight to persuade more voters.

Constructing the Survey

Since approval of the gaming measure is expected to be nearly unanimous among the Native American population, our survey focused on likely Anglo voters. Early in the survey, these respondents were asked, "How likely are you to vote for this gaming measure?" This initial response is referred to as the 'Pre-Concept' phase.

Next respondents are run through a series of positive statements regarding Oglala Sioux Gaming Initiative and asked, on a 1-to-5 scale, how much they agreed with each statement. Such statements include:

- One important reason to vote yes on the measure is the fact that Native American casinos are now among the largest employers in the areas where they are located;
- In this measure, the tribes are voluntarily dedicating 5% of the net income from Native American gaming to local schools and education programs.

Immediately after the array of statements, the survey again asks, "How Likely Are You To Vote For This Gaming Measure?' This is named 'Post-Concept'.

Given the structure of the survey, when we pool the results, will be able to see how important the different statements are to the pre and post concepts. Perhaps people who strongly disagree with Statement A have poor early opinions, but people who agree with Statement B tend to soften towards the referendum. Statement A would be a primary driver; Statement B has the potential to sway.

Basics of Regression Analysis
We discover these influences by using Regression Analysis. Essentially, Regression Analysis attempts to predict an output based on input and to determine which input variables were most critical to prediction. The outcome is called the "dependent variable" because it relies, or depends, to varying degrees on the input factors.

The outcome we are interested in is 'How Likely Are You To Vote For This Gaming Measure?' Responses are measured on a five-point scale:

- 5=Very likely to vote for gaming measure
- 4=Likely to vote for gaming measure
- 3=Neither likely nor unlikely
- 2=Unlikely to vote for gaming measure
- 1=Very unlikely to vote for gaming measure

We will use various statements as input variables. After running the regression, the statements are ranked by their p-values (a measure of their significance to the outcome). Statements with a p-value of less than 0.10 (indicating they are more than 90% likely to influence the Voting Score) will be highlighted. These represent the key drivers of the strategy.

Basis of Support—Post Concept Regression Analysis

The true foundation of support for the Gaming Measure is determined through post-concept regression. Why use post-concept? This regression captures a voter's stance after being exposed to positive attributes, reflecting their position after an attempt to "sway" their opinion.

Table 1 shows the post-concept regression.

Table 1 – Step One - Standard Regression Output

Post-Concept Support of Oglala Sioux Gaming Measure		
Native American Gaming Measure	Standardized Coefficients	
	Beta	Significance
Among Likely-to-Vote Anglo Sample		
One important reason to vote yes on the measure is the fact that Native American casinos are now among the largest employers in the areas where they are located	0.40	0.00
This measure will preserve millions of dollars in state and local taxes that are generated each year by South Dakota Native American casinos	0.35	0.00
In this measure the tribes are voluntarily dedicating 5% of the net income from Native American gaming to local schools and education programs	0.31	0.03
This measure will preserve vitally needed tribal gaming revenues which fund education, health care and housing programs on reservations	0.29	0.16
Unless this measure passes, this issue would be decided by the federal courts, not by the state of South Dakota	0.10	0.34
A yes vote on this measure will protect thousands of jobs for tribal members and other local citizens in rural counties where jobs are needed most	0.04	0.77
Oglala Sioux Casinos have pledged to signficantly fund local Black Hills Infrastruture	-0.03	0.82
This measure will help reduce unemployment and welfare on and near Native American reservations	-0.15	0.29
If this measure passes, local schools and community programs near reservations will receive millions of dollars in funds from Native American gaming revenues in the years ahead	-0.16	0.28

Examining the results, we find that three statements received significance scores below 0.10. Each of these statements pertains to factors benefiting the broader community: employment, local schools, and revenue for South Dakota's coffers. This provides a strong rationale for why voters support the measure.

Changing Minds – Layered Improvement Regression

Post-concept support is important, but what with this survey structure we can also see what *will change voters' minds in favor of the measure*. That change could be a 'Very unlikey' to 'Neither likely nor unlikely' or 'Likely to Vote' to 'Very likely to vote'.

To measure change, we create a variable which, for the sake of simplicity, we'll call *Improvement*. Improvement is created simply by the steps below:

- Improvement=Post-Concept – Pre-Concept.
- If Improvement is positive (1 or greater) we will set Improvement = 1
- Otherwise, if Improvement is zero or negative, we will set Improvement = 0.

In addition, all attributes are recoded to 1/0, with top scores 4 or 5 now simply coded as 1 while the lower scores 1,2 and 3 are now all categorized as 0. We did this to better distinguish pro-voters. The results are shown in Table 2.

Table 2 – Step Two – Layered Voter Improvement Regression

Oglala Sioux Gaming - Improvement of Gaming Measure		
Native American Gaming Measure	Standardized Coefficients	
	Beta	Significance
Among Likely-to-Vote Anglo Sample		
Oglala Sioux Casinos have pledged to signficantly fund local Black Hills Infrastruture	0.24	0.01
If this measure passes, local schools and community programs near reservations will receive millions of dollars in funds from Native American gaming revenues in the years ahead	0.23	0.02
Unless this measure passes, this issue would be decided by the federal courts, not by the state of South Dakota	0.16	0.09
A yes vote on this measure will protect thousands of jobs for tribal members and other local citizens in rural counties where jobs are needed most	0.14	0.27
This measure will help reduce unemployment and welfare on and near Native American reservations	0.06	0.61
In this measure the tribes are voluntarily dedicating 5% of the net income from Native American gaming to local schools and education programs	0.02	0.88
One important reason to vote yes on the measure is the fact that Native American casinos are now among the largest employers in the areas where they are located	0.02	0.85
This measure will preserve millions of dollars in state and local taxes that are generated each year by South Dakota Native American casinos	-0.03	0.78
This measure will preserve vitally needed tribal gaming revenues which fund education, health care and housing programs on reservations	-0.09	0.58

By recasting the regression, another picture emerges. We can see our voter's sentiments after they were exposed to the positive statements. And now, our improvement score is simplified: either 0 becomes 1 or else there was no improvement.

When we examine the results of the Improvement regression, a common theme emerges among Anglo voters: "It's good for us" and "We will not let Federal courts decide" stand out as significant. These statements are the most likely to influence voters or show improvement.

To successfully advance the Gaming initiative, we recommend that the Oglala Sioux employ both types of influencing factors: those that resonate with supporters and those that drive improvement. Often, as in this case, these two categories are not the same. For instance, if a hesitant voter isn't convinced that increasing state revenue through a new gaming facility is a strong enough reason to support it, counter with, "Would you rather leave this decision to federal judges in Washington?" This approach increases the likelihood of swaying the voter or encouraging them to reconsider their stance on the Gaming initiative.

When tracking a campaign—whether it's for a Native American casino initiative, a state senate seat, or a presidential race—it is crucial for the strategic communication team to understand how to build support. Asking why voters hold certain positions and what influenced them is essential.

Our method evaluates the potential impact of various statements, which can then be incorporated into advertising or campaign speeches. Unlike traditional techniques that assess statements based on their "stated impact," our approach emphasizes the actual effect these statements have. The key to increasing support lies in identifying which message creates the greatest positive shift, rather than simply focusing on the most liked or well-received statement.

A Streamlined, Advanced Approach to Regression – Johnson's Relative Weights

I like to say that there is nothing new under the sun statistically speaking. Almost all the math in common multivariate analyses were proven more than a century ago. Most 'new' products are a mélange of existing techniques with a simple twist.

Every so often, however, a new technique emerges that leverages prevalent methodologies with growing bandwidth of personal and cloud computing. In this piece we will introduce importance weighting, a useful technique in marketing that allows marketers to assign varying levels of importance or priority to different factors or elements within their marketing strategies. We will outline one that is gaining popularity in the marketing research world—Johnson Relative Weights.

In 2000 Jeff Johnson wrote a technical paper[1] introducing Relative Importance Weights. Until then researchers relied on traditional statistics (e.g., correlations; standardized regression weights) which are known to yield affected information concerning variable importance—especially when predictor variables are highly correlated with one another.

In Johnson Relative Weight Analysis, the focus is on determining the relative impact of each variable on the dependent variable, taking into account the influence of other variables in the model. *The relative weights of the variables are calculated based on their unique contribution to the outcome variable while considering the presence of other variables in the model.*

---

[1] Jeff W. Johnson (2000) A Heuristic Method for Estimating the Relative Weight of Predictor Variables in Multiple Regression, Multivariate Behavioral Research, 35:1, 1-19, DOI: 10.1207/S15327906MBR3501_1

The Johnson method utilizes not only standardized outcomes from regression analysis, but also correlations between the dependent and predictor variables as well as eigenvector analysis (a linear algebra matrix method) into a more nuanced 9 step technique.

In the context of political research, relative weights refer to the importance or influence of different attributes or factors on voter preferences or candidate image. Common uses for relative weights are:

- Understanding Voter Behavior
- Evaluating Public Policy Influence
- Measuring Media Influence
- Exploring Factors Behind Political Polarization
- Legislative Behavior Analysis
- Understanding Economic Inequality
- Political Strategy Analysis
- Target voter segmentation
- Marketing mix models
- Advertising campaigns

Ease of Johnson Relative Weighting

Johnson relative weighting has the ability to get granular with a large number of variables. By contrast, linear regression cannot easily handle, say, 20 variables. Differences between highly correlated variables would blur the outcome.

This is not the case with relative importance weights. Moreover, given the ease of programming, one can run the analysis across many dependent variables simply by changing one or two lines in R Statistics language code. The three lines of R-stat code (below), reads in data, and performs a relative weight analysis on a dependent variable and, in this case, 9 predictor variables.

```
# Load the 'AvWeight' dataset
data(AvWeight)

# Fit a linear regression model
model <- lm(depend ~ ., data = AvWeight)

# Perform the relative weights analysis
rel_weights <- calc.relimp(model, type = "lmg")
```

Those three lines, with slight changes of dependent variable in the code, produce Table 1, yielding a well-rounded and easy-to-replicate brand picture across 9 attributes and 6 dependent variables. Darker shades of green indicate a stronger relative weight (see Table 1, below).

Another key aspect of using JRW is that all weights, which can range from 5 to over 20 attributes, sum to 100%. This simplifies the process of identifying the winners and allows for straightforward side-by-side comparisons within the dependent variable columns.

While using Johnson's Relative Weights is fundamentally the same across various scenarios, we will demonstrate three examples to illustrate different applications of this approach. Each example will highlight a distinct context where Johnson's Relative Weights can be effectively implemented, showcasing its versatility and adaptability in achieving optimal outcomes.

Example 1 – Standing Out in a Crowded Primary

Congressional primaries can often present a challenging landscape for voters, particularly when the candidates largely converge on policy positions. In such situations, the distinctions between candidates become blurred, making it difficult for voters to discern who truly aligns with their values or offers innovative solutions. Consequently, primary elections can devolve into contests of personality or name recognition, rather than genuine debates about the future direction of policies that impact constituents' lives.

In our scenario, our candidate State Senator Frank Atwood, is one of four contenders vying for a congressional seat in Maryland's 6th congressional district. The district includes most of the western third of the state, but the bulk of its population is in the outer northern suburbs of Washington, D.C. It is a swing district.

Before challenging the incumbent, the Atwood campaign must first secure victory in the Democratic primary. To achieve this, Senator Atwood must identify his advantages and disadvantages in comparison to their intra-party rivals.

Instead of asking each respondent to rate each candidate on these 11 issues, we can determine their relative positions using a JRW construction. The survey includes the following:

On a 1-to-5 scale how likely are you to vote for [insert candidate]? Note: I have a Don't know/Don't know this candidate' as the same option.

Next you will see 11 quality-of-life statements that affect residents of Maryland. Using a scale from 1-to-10, please indicate how much each policy may influence your vote.

Table 1 - Johnson Relative Weights for Maryland's 6th District Democratic Primary

Importance vs. Intent to Vote - Maryland 6th Congressional Primary	State SenatorFrank Atwood	State Rep Renee Caldwell	County SupervisorTyson Rivers	Businesswoman Maya Greystone
Ensuring affordable healthcare for Marylanders.	12.6	17.9	5.0	7.0
Maryland focuses on improving public education quality.	0.3	7.7	13.6	11.2
Protecting the Chesapeake Bay from pollution, managing runoff, and addressing climate change.	11.5	0.0	4.5	17.7
Upgrading roads, expanding public transit options and reducing traffic congestion.	0.4	19.1	13.4	0.3
Maryland has some of the stricter gun control laws in the country.	17.4	7.5	13.8	9.6
Supporting small businesses, attracting tech and biotech industries, and ensuring economic opportunities.	8.0	11.7	1.6	8.2
Maryland has been at the forefront of discussions on police reform, criminal justice changes, and addressing racial inequalities.	13.6	6.5	7.5	8.6
Rising housing costs make affordable housing development and tenant protections.	19.9	5.9	9.0	16.2
The opioid epidemic continues to affect Maryland communities.	8.0	12.1	7.0	7.5
Ensuring fair access to voting, addressing gerrymandering issues, and maintaining transparent electoral processes.	1.0	5.4	12.5	0.8
Addressing the needs of immigrant communities and finding a balance between state policies and federal immigration laws.	7.5	6.2	12.0	12.9

For Senator Atwood's team, I would say the following. The darker the shade of green, the more the candidate is strong on this issue. The issues which are completely white are week spots. This is truth for all the candidates.

Example 2 – Johnson Relative Weights for Major Political Supporters of the Center for Urban Advancement

Table 2 presents the findings from our first example involving the Center for Urban Advancement (CUA), a nonprofit organization focused on economic and social policy research, particularly in the areas of education equity, access, and progress. CUA seeks to determine the relative importance of the attitudes perceived by its stakeholders, who are crucial for political support in Washington. In essence, CUA aims to tailor its messaging to these diverse groups to optimize its political 'punch'.

Table 2 – Johnson Relative Weights for the CUA

Attitudes Toward Education Priorities	Federal Democratic Education Influencers	Federal Republican Education Influencers	Local, state, and federal government	Nonprofits that focus on social issues, housing, education, and health	Local community organizations and grassroots groups.
Access to Quality Education	13.8	19.2	5.2	36.6	23.2
Funding for Public Schools	6.2	9.8	29.2	7.7	24.1
School Choice	10.5	26.4	5.6	5.2	6.4
Teacher Support and Compensation	14.9	2.0	23.1	22.4	12.0
Standardized Testing	2.2	1.6	4.5	9.3	1.8
Curriculum and Educational Standards	17.8	24.1	6.4	1.9	1.6
Early Childhood Education	15.5	2.5	9.8	12.4	2.0
Higher Education Affordability	18.7	9.4	3.8	3.5	8.9
Vocational and Technical Training	0.5	5.0	12.4	1.0	19.9

Here are salient points I would report to the Center for Urban Advancement at first glance:

- Your most promising supporters are local organizations and non-profits.
- The two major political parties align CUA with their own agendas. For federal Republican influencers, "School Choice" and "Curriculum" are the most significant drivers, but these policies directly conflict with CUA's overall goals.
- CUA is likely to find a more receptive audience among Democratic influencers in Washington.

Johnson's Relative Weights – Maximation of Donor Potential

In our final example, I'll share an altered case from a recent project. The Ohio State University Wexner Medical Center and College of Medicine are focusing on identifying alumni with the highest potential for financial support. The necessary data for achieving these objectives is maintained by the Ohio State University Foundation.

The Ohio State College of Medicine seeks to prioritize alumni who show a strong connection to their alma mater through engagement, career accomplishments, philanthropic contributions, and ongoing ties to the university. By focusing on these individuals, the college aims to foster meaningful alumni relationships, communicate its mission more effectively, and secure funding that enhances its ability to serve the community. They have chosen JRW to maximize the focus of their fundraising messages on key issues.

There are a few key advantages to this kind of study:

- No field costs—the Ohio State University Foundation has an enormous amount of data;
- Ease of data availability—the Ohio State University Foundation provides the data in a form that allows the analyst to shape it into an R Stat ready dataset;
- Flexibility—The model can be made to fit numerous analytics subsections. In our example, we asked the foundation for data specific for the medical center.

The initial step involves organizing the dataset by alumni donors, each of whom has contributed to the Wexner Medical Center. Since each row in the data represents a single donation, some alumni donors may have 20-30 entries. To streamline the data, we aggregate it so that each alumni donor is represented by a single row, summarizing their multiple donations. Next, we generate the following variables for analysis.

- Average Amount of Donation
- Average Frequency of Donations
- Internal Ohio State University Foundation records of events medical alumni attended.

The cleaned dataset of roughly fifty thousand alumni donors from Ohio State University Medical School is then uploaded into a dataset to be opened in R Stat for this specific analysis. The results are shown below (Figure 3).

Table 3 – Johnson's Relative for Major Donors to the Ohio State University Medical Center

Relative Importance Weights - Alumni Conbributors to the Ohio State University Hospital	
Critical Care Medicine Research	9.3
Medical Alumni Weekend	9.1
OSU Give Back Programs	8.6
Faculty Support and Development	8.5
Athletics and Sports Teams	8.4
Cancer Research	8.4
Cultural and Arts Programs	8.1
Infectious Diseases and Immunology Research	7.2
Buckeye Spirit Events	6.4
Homecoming Weekend	4.6
The Medical Center	4.3
Alumni-Patient Outreach Initiatives	4.3
Career and Mentoring Services	3.4
Alumni Family Day	2.7
Football Game Watch Parties	2.3
Scholarships/Financial Aid for Incoming Medical Students	1.9
Distinguished Medical Alumni Awards	1.4
Alumni Giving Circles	1.1

The table above presents the Johnson Relative Weighting analysis for each of the 18 Ohio State University alumni programs in the database, using donation amount and frequency as dependent variables. Among these 18 initiatives or events, the JRW highlights seven key focus areas, enabling Wexner Medical Center fundraisers to enhance fundraising outcomes and reduce outreach costs by prioritizing communications around these top seven priorities.

Exploration and Segmentation in Political Research - Latent Class and Factor Analysis
Latent Class Analysis—as commonly referred to as Factor Analysis—is a statistical method used to identify unobserved subgroups, or "latent classes," within a population based on individuals' responses to multiple observed variables. It is particularly useful in political research for uncovering hidden structures or patterns in people's attitudes, behaviors, or characteristics that traditional methods might miss. Here's how Latent Class can be applied in political research:

Factor Analysis 101
Factor analysis involves calculating correlations among all variables to determine which ones move together, suggesting they are driven by the same underlying factor. Variables that are highly correlated load onto a common factor, while those with low correlations likely belong to different factors.

Factor analysis extracts these common patterns as "factors," which represent clusters of related variables. These factors are latent constructs that might not be directly observable but explain the relationships among variables. Each factor is then interpreted based on the variables it includes, giving it a conceptual label. There are two primary types of factor analysis: exploratory, which is used when researchers don't have preconceived ideas about factor structure, and confirmatory, which tests a hypothesized factor structure.

Factor analysis can effectively handle large numbers of variables, making it particularly useful in studies where clients may provide extensive lists—such as 50-60 ice cream flavors or 40 media sources. For instance, if the data isn't from a syndicated source, a questionnaire might include a list of 40 media sources, with respondents asked to check those they regularly use. This process generates binary (1/0) variables, where

"1" indicates regular use, and "0" indicates no use. These binary variables then serve as the input for the factor analysis, enabling the technique to identify underlying patterns and groupings across a large variable set.

Below are three central examples reflecting the common utilization of Latent Class Analysis in political research.

Example 1 – Understanding Voter Behavior and Attitudes

In Figure 1, we see the factor loadings calculated and sorted. The three 'factors' are distinguished by color.

Table 1 – Latent Class Output of Factored Voting Behaviors

	Regular and Honest Voters	Media and Socially Influenced Voters	Economic and Issue Voters
Voting is an essential part of my civic duty and personal responsibility	0.72	0.04	0.19
I generally vote for candidates from my preferred political party	0.69	0.15	-0.09
I believe my vote can make a difference in the election outcome	0.54	-0.23	0.22
I have confidence that the electoral process is fair and trustworthy	0.50	0.20	0.00
I am more likely to vote for candidates whom I perceive as honest and ethical	0.47	0.32	0.13
Media coverage affects how I perceive candidates and their policies	0.37	0.72	0.34
The opinions of family and friends influence my voting choices	0.19	0.66	0.06
Policies matter more to me than a candidate's personality when I make voting decisions	0.06	0.59	0.15
I am less likely to support candidates who focus on negative campaigning against opponents	0.05	0.55	0.06
Economic conditions influence my voting decisions significantly	0.05	0.14	0.75
I am more inclined to vote for candidates who represent change rather than those advocating for continuity	0.08	-0.24	0.65
I tend to prioritize specific issues (eg, healthcare, education) over a candidate's overall platform	0.21	0.31	0.56

This straightforward example illustrates how twelve policy statements can be grouped into three distinct "families" based on their underlying correlation structure. The names of these families, displayed as column headings in Table 1, are subjective and assigned by the researcher rather than by the software. Generally, factor names are chosen to reflect the common themes or variables within each factor.

Example 2 – Analyzing Policy Preferences – Political Segmentation

Factor analysis can be used to summarize individuals' preferences on various policy issues. By identifying latent factors, researchers can simplify complex datasets and understand how preferences on specific issues relate to broader policy orientations.

Below is a poll of 2100 voters in New Jersey. They were asked to rate, on a 1-to-5 scale, how much they agreed with each of the following 12 statements. A factor analysis was run, and Figure 2 shows the rotated output data common in factor analysis.

Figure 2 – Importance Issues for New Jersey Voters

	Progressive/Liberal Leaning	Mainsteam New Jersey Issues	Conservative Leaning
New Jersey should take the lead on climate action by investing in renewable energy projects like offshore wind farms and solar power	0.60	-0.22	-0.08
The state should expand affordable housing initiatives, including rent control measures and funding for new housing developments	0.59	0.03	-0.03
New Jersey should address funding disparities in public schools by allocating more resources to lower-income districts	0.58	-0.01	0.06
The state should work to expand Medicaid and implement additional healthcare subsidies to cover uninsured and low-income residents	0.57	0.06	-0.11
New Jersey should prioritize criminal justice reform, including eliminating cash bail for non-violent offenses and investing in community programs	0.56	-0.15	-0.15
New Jersey should increase investment in renewable energy sources like wind and solar power to combat climate change	0.35	0.71	-0.07
The state should implement stronger regulations to protect the Jersey Shore and wetlands from pollution and overdevelopment	-0.08	0.69	0.01
New Jersey should provide more financial aid to make college more affordable for in-state students	-0.09	0.64	-0.20
Expanding funding for local libraries, community centers, and after-school programs should be a priority for the state	0.03	0.61	0.24
New Jersey should reduce property and income taxes to alleviate the financial burden on residents	0.03	0.51	0.69
The state should focus on creating a business-friendly environment through tax incentives	-0.08	0.41	0.68
New Jersey should increase funding for law enforcement to ensure public safety	-0.10	0.09	0.64

Assigning Segments based on the factor analysis shown in Figure 2 is performed on the factor highest loading. Three new variables are created when the software runs the analysis. Each respondent gets a factor loading (similar to a correlation coefficient). Each respondent is then grouped based on their highest factor loading. Essentially, they are placed in the segment that best matches their responses according to the strongest underlying pattern.

Table 1 – Importance Issues for New Jersey Voters

Frequency of Q-Segments	Frequency	Percent
Progressive/Liberal Leaning	845	39
Mainsteam New Jersey Issues	756	35
Conservative Leaning	543	25
Total	2144	100

Nearly 40% fell into the "Progressive Leaning" category, while approximately 25% were classified as "Conservative Leaning." The remaining 35% aligned primarily with mainstream, non-partisan New Jersey issues. These findings closely reflect the distribution of registered Democrats, Republicans, and independent voters within the state.

Example 3 – Understanding Media Consumption and Political Information – Latent Class Visualization

In this example, our client surveyed a sample of Republican-leaning voters to determine their sources of political news. Figure 3 presents a biplot illustrating the results of the latent class analysis.

The factor loading plot biplot is a visual output for factor analysis. In this biplot, both variables and cases are plotted in a two-dimensional space, where the axes represent the primary factors or components that capture the largest variance in the data.

Arrows, or vectors, represent each variable, with their direction and length indicating their correlation with the factors. Points, representing cases, are placed based on their scores on these factors.

Figure 3 – BiPlot of Factor Analysis Output – Where Do You Get Your Political News

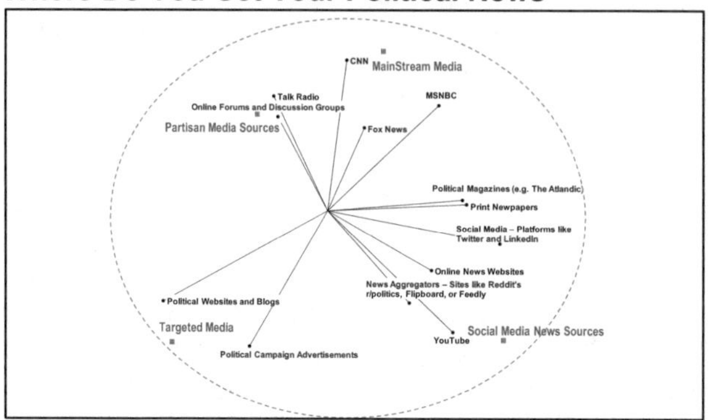

The spatial arrangement of arrows and points allows analysts to observe patterns: variables that have similar directions are positively correlated. The proximity of cases to variable vectors provides insight into how strongly each case aligns with the factors and, indirectly, with the original variables.

Think of the visual as planets and moons projected onto a unit circle. The factor names, shown in blue, represent the planets, while the various news sources are the moons. The moons orbiting a specific planet define that planet's characteristics. Moons positioned between planets can be seen as shared by multiple planets, suggesting they are influenced by several factors and are less strongly defined as distinct news sources.
At a glance, clear distinctions emerge among the news sources. Sources that do not dominate any particular factor are positioned on the map away from the blue factor heads. This suggests that the sample views political magazines, print newspapers, and platforms like Twitter/X and LinkedIn as straddling the space between mainstream media, political magazines (which are increasingly digital rather than print), and social media.

Reading the Room: Issue Optimization Approaches Through Conjoint Analysis

Conjoint analysis, a popular tool in market research, is increasingly being applied in political polling to understand voter preferences and decision-making processes. By presenting respondents with various hypothetical candidates or policy scenarios, each with different combinations of attributes (such as political stance, leadership qualities, or economic policies), conjoint analysis allows researchers to measure which factors voters prioritize. This method provides deeper insights than traditional polling, revealing how voters weigh trade-offs between competing characteristics and helping political campaigns shape messages, policy positions, or candidate profiles that resonate most with their target electorate.

Trade-off analysis enables researchers to incorporate a variety of options—such as different features, price points, and brand names—into a well-designed questionnaire. Respondents are then asked a series of questions about their interest in purchasing various products. The collected data is processed using conjoint analysis methods, which generate utility scores, providing valuable insights. These models allow researchers to simulate market conditions with impressive accuracy, offering a detailed understanding of consumer preferences and behavior.

This approach is equally applicable in political scenarios, such as evaluating a candidate's viability, uncovering the core drivers of support for issues like gun control, housing reform, or budget management, or selecting strategies for advancing legislation. When properly employed, this analysis can offer valuable insights to a governor when setting policy priorities, understanding the key concerns on voters' minds as elections approach to gauge how well a campaign's message will resonate when it reaches the public.

Basics of Political Conjoint

In the context of political science research, conjoint experiments are used to understand how different attributes (or "levels") influence decision-making, typically in voting or public opinion. Here's how conjoint levels work and examples of how they might be structured in a political context:

Candidate Attributes

These are the specific characteristics or policies of a candidate or party that voters evaluate. Common attributes include:

- Age: 35, 50, 65
- Gender: Male, Female, Non-binary
- Ethnicity: White, Black, Latino, Asian
- Political Experience: No experience, Local government, National government
- Education Level: High school, College degree, Postgraduate degree
- Occupation: Teacher, Businessperson, Lawyer, Doctor

Policy Positions

Policy positions are also key elements in conjoint experiments, helping researchers understand which specific policies voters prefer. These can vary depending on the issue:

- Taxation Policy: Lower taxes, Keep taxes the same, Increase taxes on the wealthy
- Healthcare: Universal healthcare, Public-private mix, Private healthcare
- Climate Change: Strong climate action, Moderate climate action, No action
- Immigration Policy: Open immigration, Controlled immigration, Strict immigration limits
- Economic Policy: Pro-business, Balanced regulation, Pro-worker

Party Affiliation
Party affiliation is often one of the strongest predictors of voter preferences. In conjoint experiments, voters can be asked to evaluate candidates with various party labels:
Party: Conservative, Liberal, Socialist, Green, Independent

Campaign Promises
Attributes related to campaign promises can also be important:

- Focus on Corruption: Major focus on eliminating corruption, Minor focus, No focus
- Economic Growth: Focus on rapid growth, Sustainable growth, Equality-based growth
- Education: Increase education funding, Maintain current funding, Reduce education funding

5. Personal Characteristics
Voters might also respond to personal qualities, which can be framed as level:

- Charisma: Very charismatic, Moderately charismatic, Not charismatic
- Trustworthiness: Highly trustworthy, Somewhat trustworthy, Untrustworthy
- Relatability: Very relatable, Somewhat relatable, Not relatable

Example Conjoint Setup
A conjoint experiment could show respondents two hypothetical candidates with randomly assigned levels of attributes, such as:

- Candidate 1: 50-year-old Female, Doctor, Supports universal healthcare, Pro-business economic policy, Liberal party
- Candidate 2: 40-year-old Male, Businessperson, Supports private healthcare, Pro-worker economic policy, Conservative party

Respondents would then be asked which candidate they prefer, and their preferences across multiple such combinations help researchers understand which attributes and levels have the most impact on decision-making.

This chapter will demonstrate two of the most effective applications of conjoint analysis in political research. We will explore two specific constructs of conjoint that are particularly well-suited for politics. These methods can be easily conducted over the phone or online, keeping costs and timelines efficient—especially important for flash polls. Additionally, the results can be conveniently segmented by key voter groups, allowing for comparisons and an assessment of the relative importance of issues within each group.

First Model: Assessing Levels of Preference

The first model examines various levels of the day's most important issues, aiming to assess the preferences between them. The goal is to build a simulation that enables political strategists to determine the ideal policy mix or evaluate how different scenarios impact approval ratings. In this example, we will focus on three key voting groups and their positions on three political issues in the fictional state of Arizona. These groups and issues are outlined below.

Table 1 – Summary of Key Voter Groups and Three Main Issues Being Polled in the Arizona Gubernational Race

Key Voter Groups	Issues
Young Adults 18-24	Funding Water Security
Working Adults 25-54	Immigration and Border Security
Retirement on the Radar 55+	Addressing Housing Affordability

For each issue, varying levels are tested.

Funding Water Security
- Mandatory Increased Water Conservation – Rise in the price of water
- Investment in Water Infrastructure - Spending state funds to improve Arizona's water infrastructure
- Agricultural Water Reform – A water tax on agricultural institutions

Immigration and Border Security Measures
- Increased border security
- Comprehensive immigration reform and path to citizenship
- Positive economic implications of immigration workers to industries like agriculture and construction.

Addressing Housing Affordability
- Expand affordable housing development
- Zoning reform for inclusive development
- Deregulation to increase housing supply

For conjoint analysis to be most effective, a computer-generated survey plan is used to ensure the results are statistically stable. This process, known as orthogonal design, optimizes the model's output. The term orthogonal generally means things that are independent or uncorrelated. When applied to design, it often refers to elements or systems that *do not interfere with each other and can function independently.*

To administer the poll the respondent to rate a generic gubernational candidate given the following conditions on a finite scale, say 1 to 10. A sample question would look like this. *"On a 1-to-10 scale, how likely are you to support a candidate with the following three policy positions: Mandatory increased water conservation, comprehensive immigration reform and path to citizenship, and zoning reform for inclusive development.*

In the above case, with three issues each containing three levels, the respondent would be asked to rate between 9-15 choice scenarios. Below is an example of how a three orthogonally designed choice scenarios might look:

Table 2 – Example of Three Political Scenarios

Funding Water Security	Immigration and Border Security	Addressing Housing Affordability
Investment in water infrastructure	Positive economic implications of immigration workers to industries like agriculture and construction.	Expand affordable housing development
Agricultural water tax	Increased border security	Deregulation to increase housing supply
Mandatory increased water conservation	Comprehensive immigration reform and path to citizenship	Zoning reform for inclusive development

In our example, each respondent would be asked to rate nine similar questions.

The output has two levels, the first is an importance for each issue. Next, a second utility score for each *level* of each attribute.
Figure 1 summarizes the aggregate results of the importance of each issue broken down by voter group.

Figure 1 - Relative Importance of Issues Among Key Voter Groups

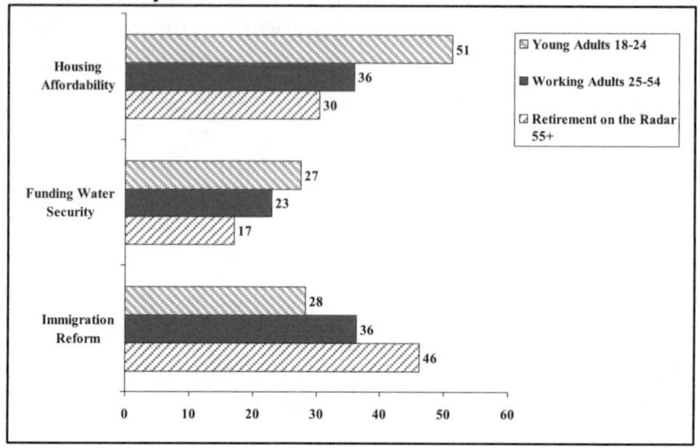

Younger voters are primarily focused on housing affordability, as they face greater challenges in finding a place to live. In contrast, water security is a less pressing issue for them, especially compared to older voters, who prioritize stricter border reforms. These older voters are more concerned with immigration control and favor tougher measures on border security.

Table 3 presents the utility scores for each attribute across the entire population—though the conjoint analysis generates scores for each voter group.

There are two main ways to interpret these figures. The first is through a quick comparison to evaluate the relative strength of each utility score. For the full population, it's clear that Housing Affordability is the top attribute, but it varies widely among our key voter groups.

Table 3 – Raw Conjoint Utilities Among Key Voter Groups

Housing Affordability	Total Sample	Young Adults 18-24	Working Adults 25-54	Retirement on the Radar 55+
Expand affordable housing development	0.84	0.93	1.21	0.37
Zoning reform for inclusive development	0.88	1.72	0.54	0.37
Deregulation to increase housing supply	0.82	0.63	0.82	1.01
Funding Water Security		**Young Adults 18-24**	**Working Adults 25-54**	**Retirement on the Radar 55+**
Investment in water infrastructure	0.58	0.86	0.40	0.49
Agricultural water tax	0.39	0.47	0.27	0.43
Mandatory increased water conservation	0.42	0.32	0.73	0.20
Immigration Reform		**Young Adults 18-24**	**Working Adults 25-54**	**Retirement on the Radar 55+**
Increased border security	0.65	0.20	0.80	0.95
Comprehensive immigration reform and path to citizenship	0.42	0.67	0.31	0.26
Positive economic implications of immigration workers to industries like agriculture and construction.	0.60	0.80	0.63	0.37

Using total utility scores from conjoint analysis allows campaigns to make data-driven decisions by evaluating voter preferences for different policy configurations. By adding the utility scores of various attribute levels (such as housing, water, and immigration), campaigns can identify which combinations yield the highest total utility, indicating the most preferred positions overall and among specific voter segments when filters are applied. This enables campaigns to prioritize key issues and tailor their messaging to resonate with the preferences of targeted voter groups. Table 4 shows us the maximized policy positions among the three voter groups.

Table 4 – Maximized Issue Positions Among Key Voter Groups

Key Group	Young Adults 18-24	Working Adults 25-54	Retirement on the Radar 55+
Housing Affordability	Zoning reform for inclusive development	Expand affordable housing development	Deregulation to increase housing supply
Key Group	**Young Adults 18-24**	**Working Adults 25-54**	**Retirement on the Radar 55+**
Funding Water Security	Investment in water infrastructure	Mandatory increased water conservation	Investment in water infrastructure
Key Group	**Young Adults 18-24**	**Working Adults 25-54**	**Retirement on the Radar 55+**
Immigration Reform	Positive economic implications of immigration workers to industries like agriculture and construction.	Increased border security	Increased border security

This summary table plays a crucial role in campaign planning by influencing several key factors. The importance of understanding your audience cannot be overstated. Whether crafting stump speeches, planning media strategies, or scheduling events for crowds influenced by their priority issues, the primary objective of using conjoint polling is to identify and maximize positions that resonate with key voter groups.

Second Model: Ranking Key Issues Using Conjoint Importance Percentages

The second variation involves using conjoint analysis to understand preferences without directly asking respondents to rank or prioritize policies. "Inferred rankings" are considered better than "stated rankings" in some contexts because they are often seen as more reliable, reflecting real behavior or preferences rather than self-reported data.

In the second variation of conjoint analysis, each issue has only two levels: it is either included in the campaign, speech, or advertisement, or it is not. This differs from other models where an issue might have three different variations or degrees of emphasis.

For instance, as Governor Tony Evers of Wisconsin prepares his State of the State address, his team seeks to rank six key issues that matter most to Wisconsin voters. How should he prioritize these challenges to ensure the greatest impact with the public? These issues are shown in Figure 5.

Table 5 – Six Key Issues Being Considered for the Governor's Speech

Policy	Key Policy Positions for Inclusion in Speech
Healthcare	Expanding Medicaid, addressing healthcare affordability, and improving access to services in rural areas.
Education	Public school funding, teacher retention, and policies around school choice and vouchers.
Economy and Jobs	Job creation, workforce development, and supporting small businesses, particularly in manufacturing and agriculture.
Public Safety and Criminal Justice	Police reform, gun control, and reducing crime rates in urban areas.
Agriculture and Rural Development	Supporting Wisconsin's dairy industry, rural infrastructure improvements, and addressing challenges facing family farms.
Environmental Policy	Protecting the state's natural resources, addressing water contamination issues, and combating climate change through renewable energy initiatives.

For six issues, the computer generates eight choice scenarios using a statistically valid orthogonal design, each presenting different combinations of issues. For instance, one question might be: "If the governor's State of the State address focused on public safety, gun control and environmental protection, how interested would you be (on a scale of 1 to 7)?" Another example could be: "In his State of the State address, Governor Tony Evers plans to emphasize 1) stopping unchecked development in Wisconsin, 2) improving classroom teaching quality, and 3) protecting the environment. How strongly would you be interested (on a scale of 1 to 7)?"

The output would look like Figure 2, which is a summary of relative importance scores once the analysis is complete.

Figure 2 – Relative Importance of Major Issues in Wisconsin

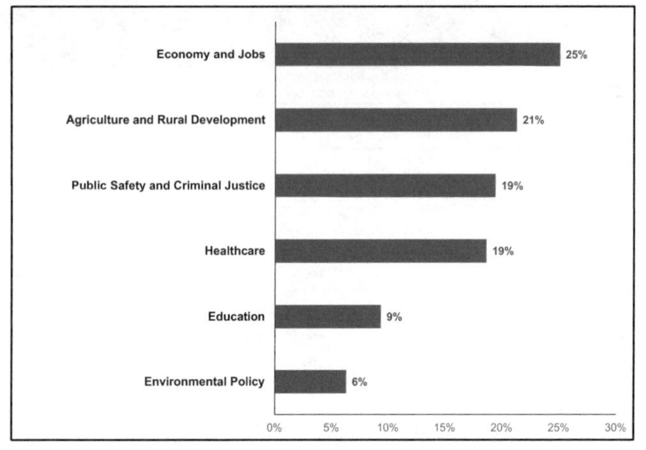

The conjoint analysis shows that Wisconsinites are primarily concerned with the state's economy, the agriculture industry, public safety, and healthcare. These major issues should be central to the governor's address. If time permits, he can also address education and environmental policy.

Conjoint analysis is one of the many statistical techniques Multivariate Solutions offers to enhance existing polls and provide strategists with deeper insights for planning. Not all campaign advertising dollars are equally effective—some generate significantly more impact than others. If strategists could know in advance which dollars to spend and which audiences to target, their chances of success would greatly improve. Conjoint analysis can serve as that predictive tool, offering valuable foresight for decision-making.

Perceptual Mapping in Politics: Visualizing Influence and Ideology

Campaigns begin with a candidate. In the beginning each candidate, regardless of party or of the office sought, must first consider some very basic questions: Who am I politically? What do I want to achieve? Why I am uniquely qualified? The answers to these questions define the candidate's public profile, or political brand.

Campaign research starts with a baseline survey – asking carefully worded questions of a scientifically selected sample of people by phone, online or face-to-face – to analyze the issue environment, demographics, party affiliation, and relative positive and negative images of the candidates.

The polling data and research must be analyzed more deeply to facilitate clear, understandable, effective and easily implemented strategic and tactical decisions.

This article will explore the use of a political visual, the perceptual map. This visual, often using in branding and advertising research, can be employed to demonstrate a candidate's early position, movement as the campaign progresses, and the identification of 'wedge' issues to focus on to determine what swings undecided voters.

Perceptual Maps - Basics

Perceptual mapping is a graphical marketing technique that visually displays the perceptions of voters. Typically the position of a product, product line, brand, or company is displayed relative to their competition.

I like to use the following analogy to explain a perceptual map. Candidates are like planets, issues are like moons. Proximity to a candidate indicates a strong association to that candidate.

The Initial Picture - Mapping The Candidates On The Issues

Early in the survey, respondents are asked for whom they intend to vote. Later, they are shown an array of issues. In our fictional example, eleven key descriptions were shown about the major candidates vying for the Democratic Presidential Nomination in 2008. The survey can be designed two ways, either:

- Numerical scale (e.g. 1-to-10) 'How much does this attribute describe [candidate]?
- Applies to [candidate] (Yes/No)

The advantage of using a numerical scale is that it allows more variability in the data, and would more likely produce a clearer map. However, in a crowded primary, when there are several candidates, it is more efficient to have respondents check off candidate descriptions, particularly if the survey is done over the phone.

Below is the candidate picture as the campaign heads into full swing. This initial perceptual map has an added dimension—the size of the candidate's planet represents their current support. Thus, the map illustrates not only the level of support, but the basis of support as well.

Figure 1 – Correspondence Map - Poll of 2008 Democratic Candidates

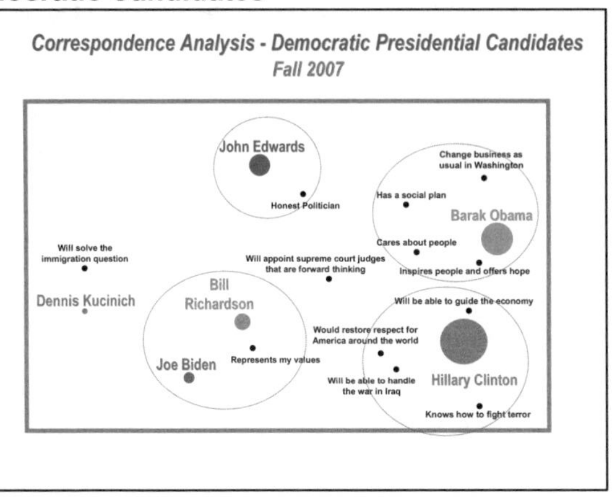

At this point in the campaign, Hillary Clinton is leading, with a solid basis of 'experience and competency'. Her main opponent, Barak Obama—current President of the United States—is seen as a more human candidate whose strength lies in change, social responsibility, and inspiration.

John Edwards's main support is honesty, while dark horse candidates Bill Richardson and Joe Biden's support lies mainly with people who identify with them personally.

The General Election - Finding Wedge Issues:
Wedge issues are those which are owned by neither party, but can sway undecided voters. The survey construction for a perceptual map is similar to the one above.

- Numerical scale (e.g. 1-to-10) 'How important is this issue to you?'
- Applies to a your ideal candidate (Yes/No)
- Issues near 'Undecided' are *wedge* issues.

The resulting perceptual map looks like this:

Figure 2 – Correspondence Map – Determining Wedge Issues for Major Party and Undecided Voters

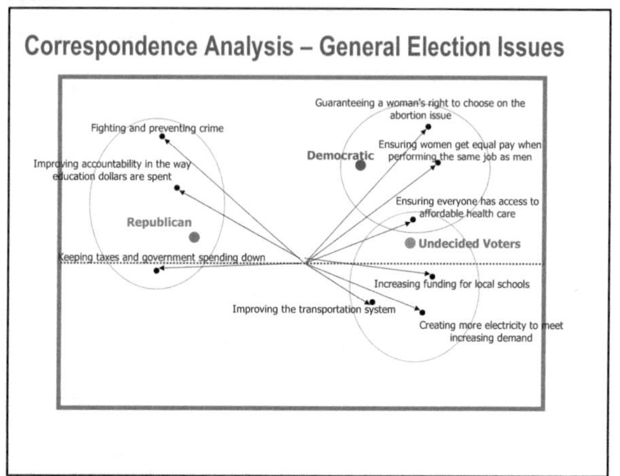

Examining the map, there are no surprises. The Democrat key attributes are in line with core Democratic issues. The Republican challenger is running on Republican standards. *Defend your ground*. Repeat the party standards to keep the base enthusiastic.

In this local race, there are four wedge issues – that is, four issues that no party candidate owns. One, 'Affordable Health Care', stands between Democratic and Undecided. If your candidate is the Democrat, own this.

Three other issues, 'Increasing funding for local schools, 'Improving the transportation system,' and 'Creating more electricity to meet increasing demand', are up for grabs. These are the issues upon which the outcome will most likely be decided.

The advantage to using perceptual maps is that they are easily understood. Any political strategist or campaign manager can glance at the visual and immediately grasp the strategic implications no matter their statistical background. The analysis can be filtered by various voter blocks to produce multiple maps. Equally essential, survey design is simple and easy to field – in the polling business, length of questionnaire is time, and time is money.

Voter Behavior Forecasting in Political Studies: Logistic Regression and Odds Ratio Insights

Logistic regression is a powerful statistical tool often used in political polling to model and predict binary outcomes, such as whether a person will vote for Candidate A or Candidate B based on various predictors. It is particularly useful when the dependent variable is categorical, as it allows researchers to assess the relationship between several independent variables (demographics, political preferences, etc.) and a binary outcome (e.g., "Vote" or "Not Vote").

How Logistic Regression Applies in Political Polling

Logistic regression predicts probabilities of binary outcomes (e.g., yes/no, Democrat/Republican). In polling, it might estimate the likelihood that a respondent will vote for a specific candidate based on their characteristics (age, education, etc.).

Independent variables can include voter demographics, geographic information, past voting behavior, and opinions on issues. For example, age, gender, income, and party affiliation could be used to predict a voter's behavior.

Initial Logistic Regression

In logistic regression, the raw beta coefficients represent the change in the log-odds of the dependent variable for a one-unit change in the predictor variable, while holding all other variables constant. These beta coefficients indicate how strongly each predictor is associated with the likelihood of the outcome. However, because the raw betas are expressed in log-odds, they are not intuitively interpretable for most real-world applications. To make the results more understandable, we often transform the raw beta values into odds ratios by taking the exponential of each coefficient.

This transformation allows us to express the results in terms of odds, making it easier to interpret the magnitude and direction of the predictor's impact.

The regression provides coefficients for each predictor variable, indicating how much each variable contributes to the odds of the outcome. The coefficients are usually transformed into odds ratios (via the exponential function), which describe the increase or decrease in the likelihood of an outcome per unit change in a predictor variable. Logistic regression outputs a log-odds value that is then converted into a probability. For example, if the model predicts that a respondent has a log-odds of 0.5 of voting for a candidate, that corresponds to a probability of about 62%.

By converting the raw beta coefficients into odds ratios, logistic regression provides a more interpretable way to understand how different factors influence the probability of an event.

Table 1 – Initial Logistic Regression Output for Sofia Vallen[2]

Vote for 'Sofia Vallen' Logistic Regression			
Regression Output	**Status**	**Regression Beta**	**Sum (b*c)**
Gender 1=Male 2=Female	2	2.67	5.34
Marital Status 1=Married/0=Not Married	1	2.10	2.10
College Graduate 1=Yes, 0=No	1	1.80	1.80
Working Woman in House 1=Yes, 0=No	1	1.76	1.76
Urban 1=Urban, 0=Not urban	1	1.65	1.65
Housing 1=Own, 0=Rent	1	0.80	0.80
Credit Card Debt 1=Yes, 0=No	0	-0.86	0.00
Equation Constant			-10.000
Sum			**3.446**
Odds Ratio ($1/(1+e^{-z})$)	**0.97**		
Predicted Likelihood of Voting for Sofia	**97%**		

---

[2] Attributes shaded yellow are statistically significant at the 95% level

Support for Sofia Vallen in our model is primarily influenced by factors such as gender, marital status, education level, the presence of a working woman in the household, and whether the residence is located in an urban or non-urban area.

Plugging in simulators to transform logistic regression betas into odds ratios can provide a dynamic way to explore the relationship between predictor variables and outcomes. Simulators, such as interactive dashboards or statistical tools, allow users to input different beta values and instantly see the corresponding odds ratios. This transformation, as discussed earlier, involves taking the exponential of each beta coefficient, and simulators make this process user-friendly, allowing real-time manipulation of the input data.

In our initial example, we calculate the odds for a college-educated, working woman who resides in an urban area, is married, owns her home, and has no credit card debt.

Example 1 – Educated, Urban, Married Working Woman

This is Sofia Vallen's base. The chance of this voter is to vote for her is estimated at 97%.

In the second example, we adjust two demographic factors. The voter is now male and has some credit card debt. All the rest of the input is the same. Sofia's estimated support level drops significantly to 48%.

Example 2 – Educated, Urban Married, Man with Working Wife and Credit Card Debt

Vote for 'Sofia Vallen' Logistic Regression			
Regression Output	**Answer**	**Regression Beta**	**Sum (b*c)**
Gender 1=Male 2=Female	1	2.67	2.67
Marital Status 1=Married/0=Not Married	1	2.10	2.10
College Graduate 1=Yes, 0=No	1	1.80	1.80
Working Woman in House 1=Yes, 0=No	1	1.76	1.76
Urban 1=Urban, 0=Not urban	1	1.65	1.65
Housing 1=Own, 0=Rent	1	0.80	0.80
Credit Card Debt 1=Yes, 0=No	1	-0.86	-0.86
Equation Constant			-10.000
Sum			**-0.084**

Odds Ratio (1/(1+e^{-z})	**0.48**
Predicted Likelihood of Voting for Sofia	**48%**

A non-urban married man without a college education, despite having some economic advantages (such as owning his home, no credit card debt, and a working wife), still has only a 6% likelihood of supporting Sofia Vallen.

Example 3 – Non-College Educated, Married Non-Urban Man Who Owns His Home

Vote for 'Sofia Vallen' Logistic Regression			
Regression Output	**Answer**	**Regression Beta**	**Sum (b*c)**
Gender 1=Male 2=Female	1	2.67	2.67
Marital Status 1=Married/0=Not Married	1	2.10	2.10
College Graduate 1=Yes, 0=No	0	1.80	0.00
Working Woman in House 1=Yes, 0=No	1	1.76	1.76
Urban 1=Urban, 0=Not urban	0	1.65	0.00
Housing 1=Own, 0=Rent	1	0.80	0.80
Credit Card Debt 1=Yes, 0=No	0	-0.86	0.00
Equation Constant			-10.000
Sum			**-2.673**

Odds Ratio (1/(1+e^{-z})	**0.06**
Predicted Likelihood of Voting for Sofia	**6%**

Batch Fit and Segmentation

Batch fit and segmentation are two important concepts in logistic regression that can significantly enhance model performance. Batch fit refers to the process of fitting the logistic regression model using the entire dataset at once.

In this method, the optimization algorithm uses the entire dataset to determine the best-fit coefficients for the predictor variables. The key advantage of batch fitting is its stability, particularly for small to medium-sized datasets, as it reduces noise and leads to more consistent outcomes. It is important to remember that when building a model, all variables included in that model must also be present in the dataset being evaluated or scored.

Segmentation, in this case, entails drawing lines of support and separating them into groups. For example, the Vallen team wants 'Key Supporters' to be at a 75% likelihood of voting for their candidate, or higher. Persuadables are between 40%-74%. Unlikeliest are below 40% chance of voting for their candidate.

Each segment is treated as a separate entity. This approach improves the precision and interpretability of the model, particularly in diverse datasets where distinct segments display different behaviors. Segmentation is particularly valuable in marketing, political polling, and customer analytics, where tailored media and message strategies are necessary for different subgroups.

Logistic regression is a powerful and versatile tool for political polling, enabling analysts to predict voter behavior and understand the key factors influencing election outcomes. Its ability to model binary outcomes, such as vote choices, makes it especially valuable in political research.

Using a mix of demographic, geographic, and behavioral variables, logistic regression sheds light on how likely voters are to back particular candidates or policies. Beyond that, its role in segmentation sharpens its predictive power, enabling focused analyses of different voter groups. In the ever-changing world of political polling, logistic regression stands as a cornerstone for crafting informed, data-driven strategies in campaigns and political planning.

Comparative Discriminant Analysis—Demographic and Media Consumption Analysis of Voter Bases in Multiparty Electoral Systems

Political parties often define themselves through specific ideologies, policy priorities, and core values that reflect the interests and aspirations of their base. They use these definitions to distinguish themselves from their opponents, build a clear brand identity, and appeal to particular voter demographics. By highlighting key issues—such as economic policy, social values, or governance approaches—they aim to create a cohesive message that resonates with their supporters and guides their stance on current political debates, helping to shape their public image and drive support during elections.

Do the voters see the parties the same as the parties see themselves? The short answer, not always. Voters often perceive political parties differently than the parties see themselves, as public perception is influenced by various factors such as media portrayal, campaign advertisements, and individual experiences.

Multiparty elections are more common in parliamentary systems than in the American political landscape, especially during general elections which are largely dominated by two major parties. In parliamentary systems, proportional representation enables multiple political parties to gain seats in the legislature, reflecting a wider range of political perspectives. This structure encourages coalition-building, as it's uncommon for a single party to achieve a majority. While this methodology is primarily linked to parliamentary systems, it can also be effectively applied to crowded primary elections within the two-party framework of the United States.

Research indicates that sophisticated political analysis offers more accurate insights into a party's true identity than its official platforms or advertisements. This article will present a streamlined multivariate method to analyze the differences and similarities between voter perceptions and party self-definitions. It will also highlight the ease of reporting these findings to media teams and political managers for strategic application.

Basics of Discriminant Analysis
Discriminant analysis is a statistical technique used to classify observations into predefined groups based on their characteristics. It identifies the optimal combination of predictor variables that best distinguish between groups, maximizing their differences.

The method involves developing one or more discriminant functions, which estimate the probability of each observation belonging to a specific group.

This technique is widely used in fields such as finance, market segmentation, customer profiling, psychology, education, sports science, criminology, and, notably, political and public affairs polling.

Primary Features of Comparative Discriminant Analysis
Comparative discriminant analysis (CDA) involves conducting *repeated analyses* while *altering only the dependent variable*.

This approach allows researchers to describe membership in various categories—such as political parties, voter blocs, or ideological groups—based on observed variables like demographics, voting patterns, issue importance, and leadership qualities. This method is particularly useful in understanding voter behavior, political polarization, and the effects of various social, economic, or cultural influences on political outcomes.

Indian Elections
As an example, we will use a mock election in the largest democracy in the world—India. As of the most

recent data, 36 political parties are represented in the 18th Lok Sabha (the lower house of India's national parliament), which was elected in 2024. These include both national and regional parties. The composition changes with each election and as parties form coalitions or merge.

The results of India's general elections for the 18th Lok Sabha, held from April to June 2024, were announced on June 4th and 5th, 2024. The primary competitors were two major alliances: the incumbent National Democratic Alliance (NDA)[3], led by the Bharatiya Janata Party (BJP), and the opposition Indian National Developmental Inclusive Alliance (I.N.D.I.A.), led by the Indian National Congress.[4]

Table 1 – Top 6 Parties in the Lok Sabha After the 2024 Election

Political Party	Political Position	Number of Seats in Last Election (2024)	Alliance
Bharatiya Janata Party (BJP)	Right-Wing, Conservative, And Nationalist - Currently The Ruling Party	240	Government
Indian National Congress (INC)	Centre-Left	97	I.N.D.I.A
Samajwadi Party (SP)	Centre-Left, Socialist	37	I.N.D.I.A
All India Trinamool Congress (AITC)	Centre-Left, Populist, Regionalism.	29	I.N.D.I.A
Dravida Munnetra Kazhagam (DMK)	Centre-Left, Dravidianism, Social Democracy	22	I.N.D.I.A
Telugu Desam Party (TDP)	Centre-Right, Regionalism	16	Government

Comparative discriminant analysis provides researchers with insights into the demographic and psychographic profiles of all parties involved in an election. This encompasses factors such as where they reside, how they consume news, and which social media platforms are favored by party supporters.

---

[3] The **National Democratic Alliance (NDA)** is a coalition of political parties in India, led by the **Bharatiya Janata Party (BJP)**.
[4] The Indian National Developmental Inclusive Alliance (I.N.D.I.A.) is a broad coalition of multiple political parties in India, spearheaded by the Indian National Congress, the country's largest opposition party.

Construction of the Discriminant Dependent Variables

The discriminant dependent variable is formed by combining predictor variables into a linear function to maximize differences between categories. Discriminant analysis determines coefficients that improve group separation, creating a discriminant function to classify observations into predefined groups, enhancing prediction accuracy.

In this example, we analyze voters from six major Indian political parties. The dependent variables are calculated as follows: if a person votes for the BJP party, their BJP-dependent variable is assigned a value of 1; otherwise, it is 0.

This process is repeated for each of the six parties, resulting in *six dependent variables* that are used in the analysis.

Creation of the Independent Variables

The strength of comparative discriminant analysis is its ability to leverage multiple facets of the survey to uncover the motivations behind voter behavior. For each political party, a separate analysis is conducted, providing a comprehensive roadmap. Rather than offering a single set of directions, this approach yields distinct, multi-layered descriptions of the political actors. Table 2 presents the four-dimensional comparative arrays.

Table 2 – Four Comparative Discriminant Analysis Arrays

	Number of Items/Attributes	Number of Descriptor Variables
Demographics	12	12
Indian Issue Importance	11	11
Indian Political Party Profiles	9	9
Indian Leadership Qualities	15	15

In a comparative discriminant, it is not unusual to use six or seven different sections of a survey. Additionally, questionnaires can be split, or certain arrays can be excluded from different surveys, which helps to control both the cost and quality of a long survey. To illustrate this, we will simplify our analysis of the Indian National Election by focusing on a demographic table and three candidate arrays.

The demographic variables included in the initial analysis are listed below.

- Education
- Employment
- Age
- Income
- Gender
- India Regions
- Mobile phone only
- News - Television, Radio, Newspapers
- News - Internet
- Social Media 1=Yes, 0=No
- Use Indian Social Media More Than International

Table 3 – Discriminant Scores for Demographic Variables

	Bharatiya Janata Party (BJP)	Indian National Congress (INC)	Samajwadi Party (SP)	All India Trinamool Congress (AITC)	Dravida Munnetra Kazhagam (DMK)	Telugu Desam Party (TDP)
Education 0=High School or less, 1=Vocational/University	-0.04	-0.04	-0.29	0.00	-0.36	0.26
Upper Caste/Business Elite	0.64	0.19	0.07	-0.57	0.06	0.49
Supervisory/Managerial Workers/Professional/Executive	0.52	-0.08	-0.51	0.48	-0.51	0.28
Family Business/Small Merchant/Skilled Workers	0.03	-0.02	0.66	0.15	0.62	0.17
Unemployed/Housewife/Student	-0.42	0.38	0.06	-0.41	0.07	0.16
General work/Farming/Independent/Unskilled Workers	0.26	0.52	0.59	0.72	0.27	-0.63
Age 1=18-24, 2=25-34, 3=35-54, 4=55+	0.03	-0.35	0.12	-0.09	0.13	-0.09
Income, 0=Poorest 25% <B24K, 1=Middle 65%, 2=Wealthiest 10% B40K+	0.08	0.50	-0.16	0.12	-0.01	-0.21
Gender 1=Male, 0=Female	0.17	-0.22	0.00	0.11	-0.09	0.07
Regional Party 1=Yes, 0=No	-0.42	0.18	-0.25	-0.51	0.31	0.41
News - Television, Radio, Newspapers	0.04	-0.01	0.66	-0.02	0.32	0.55
News - Internet	0.41	-0.55	0.07	-0.20	-0.67	0.35
Social Media 1=Yes, 0=No	0.04	0.12	0.04	0.13	0.05	0.05
Use Indian Social Media More Than International	0.30	0.17	0.31	0.17	0.43	0.43

Examining the table, we find that the key demographic descriptors, whether positive or negative, reveal how respondents perceive the party they intend to vote for. A negative coefficient can be most easily understood by placing a "NOT" in front of the variable descriptor.

For example, we can describe the key demographic descriptors of the dominant BJP party as such:

- The party of the elites and professional class
- NOT the party of the unemployed
- NOT a regional party
- A large number of BJP voters get their news from the internet. In a country like India that is not a given.

Table 4 – Discriminant Scores for Centrality of Indian Political Issues

	Bharatiya Janata Party (BJP)	Indian National Congress (INC)	Samajwadi Party (SP)	All India Trinamool Congress (AITC)	Dravida Munnetra Kazhagam (DMK)	Telugu Desam Party (TDP)
Economic Growth & Job Creation	0.08	-0.02	0.51	-0.13	0.05	0.06
Education System Revamp	-0.31	-0.17	-0.24	0.65	0.38	0.13
Agriculture & Rural Development	0.18	0.39	-0.34	-0.02	0.09	0.19
Empowerment of Women & Gender Equality	-0.20	0.05	0.43	0.32	-0.46	-0.43
Environmental Protection & Sustainable Development	-0.02	0.37	0.02	-0.15	-0.24	0.24
Federalism & State Rights	-0.34	0.33	-0.16	0.68	0.04	0.72
Digital Transformation & Technology Access	0.34	-0.21	-0.23	0.09	0.25	0.10
Urban Development & Public Services	0.40	0.09	-0.10	-0.02	-0.03	-0.33
National Security & Defense	0.46	-0.42	-0.09	-0.29	-0.03	0.04
Corruption & Governance Reform	-0.47	-0.14	-0.12	-0.60	0.52	0.01
Poverty Eradication & Social Justice	-0.01	-0.01	0.50	-0.23	0.06	0.72

Let's assume we are working with the largest opposition party, the INC. This table allows us to draw contrasts at the statistical description of the ruling BJP party as well as descriptors for the other 4 parties (out of total of 35 parties represented in the Lok Sabha. We know that the ruling party is:

- Strong on national issues, is focused on urban India, and a strong defense.
- Weak on education, Indian states rights, and viewed as corrupt.

We can also assume that our client, the leftist INC, is:

- Strong on agricultural, environment, and state rights
- Weak on national security.

Table 5 – Discriminant Scores Indian Leadership Qualities

	Bharatiya Janata Party (BJP)	Indian National Congress (INC)	Samajwadi Party (SP)	All India Trinamool Congress (AITC)	Dravida Munnetra Kazhagam (DMK)	Telugu Desam Party (TDP)
Integrity	-0.40	0.13	-0.15	-0.21	-0.01	-0.04
Visionary Thinking	-0.03	0.30	-0.12	0.43	0.45	-0.46
Empathy and Compassion	-0.01	0.41	0.31	0.21	-0.49	0.00
Adaptability	-0.09	0.26	0.45	-0.04	-0.47	-0.22
Strong Communication Skills	0.33	-0.34	0.14	-0.06	0.12	0.07
Decisiveness	0.49	0.19	-0.09	-0.18	0.33	0.49
Cultural Sensitivity	-0.35	0.10	0.08	-0.09	-0.41	0.22
Problem-Solving Abilities	-0.20	-0.36	0.04	-0.31	0.00	0.34
Inclusiveness	-0.32	0.46	-0.16	-0.40	-0.06	-0.46
Resilience	0.51	0.25	-0.29	-0.37	-0.20	0.28
Grassroots Connectivity	0.12	-0.06	-0.36	0.33	0.23	-0.20
Collaborative Approach	-0.45	0.24	-0.16	0.19	0.13	0.36
Accountability and Transparency	-0.50	-0.04	0.16	-0.30	0.09	0.08
Courage and Willpower	0.08	-0.04	-0.22	0.08	-0.35	-0.27
Commitment to Social Justice	0.14	0.45	0.01	-0.24	-0.06	-0.20

The longer a political party remains in power, the more it risks becoming unpopular due to a combination of factors. Over time, voters may grow disillusioned with unmet promises, stagnation in leadership, or scandals that accumulate as a party holds power. Policies that once seemed innovative may become outdated, while the opposition gains traction by offering fresh ideas and critiquing the government's performance. The natural cycle of political fatigue sets in as the electorate seeks change, variety, or new solutions to persistent problems.

Reviewing Table 5 reveals that India's governing party, the BJP, is not immune to voter discontent. According to respondents, the party is not perceived as honest, inclusive, collaborative, or transparent, but it is regarded as effective.

In contrast, the main opposition party, the INC, is seen as empathetic, inclusive, and committed to social justice—traits that stand in opposition to the BJP.

However, the data suggests that while the INC may offer a distinct alternative in terms of values, it is not viewed as particularly effective as a governing force.

Comparative Discriminant Analysis is a robust statistical method that elevates the sophistication of political polling. Unlike conventional approaches that focus solely on measuring voter preferences, CDA enables pollsters to categorize voters into distinct groups using multiple variables, such as demographics, voting history, and political attitudes.

Comparative discriminant analysis's ability to identify patterns and predict voting behavior makes it invaluable for political strategists. By analyzing complex relationships between independent variables, CDA helps in forecasting election outcomes more accurately than simple trend analysis. It also enables campaigns to tailor their outreach efforts to specific voter groups, improving the precision of micro-targeting strategies.

Quadrants in Political Research – Kano and Competitive Issue Matrices

Matrix analysis plays a critical role in political polling by segmenting voters based on two or three key dimensions, such as policy preferences and candidate favorability. By analyzing these segments, campaigns can tailor messaging, allocate resources efficiently, and refine outreach strategies.

Matrices also highlight shifts in voter sentiment over time, providing actionable insights for adapting campaign tactics. Its clarity and precision make it a powerful tool for targeting voters and maximizing political influence in competitive electoral environments.

Example 1 – Political Kano Analysis

Political Kano Analysis integrates the Kano model of customer satisfaction with a quadrant framework to assess political strategies or policy initiatives. By categorizing voter preferences or policy attributes into four key Kano dimensions, this analysis plots them against axes of derived importance and stated issue importance.

Survey Design

We chart the issues voters say are important on a 1-to-7 scale This is plotted on the X-Axis.

We evaluate each candidate on these issues together with individual's 'intent to vote'. This is termed derived importance.

- Derived importance is regression analysis that reflects the strength of association between a candidate's policy positions and the likelihood of voter support, as indicated by the statistical weights or coefficients assigned to various policies in the model.
- The statistical weights are normalized and then graphed on the Y-Axis.

Our example is demonstrated in Figure 1.

Figure 1 – Kano Quadrant Analysis Output

Stated versus Derived Importance Analysis

DERIVED ISSUE IMPORTANCE

	Low (Stated)	High (Stated)
High	***Constituent Unmet Needs (Wedge Issues)*** Health Care Abortion National Security Tax Policy Social Security	***Campaign Key Drivers*** Education Environment Immigration Iraq & "War on Terror" Change
Low	***Indifference Points*** Budget & Spending Corporations/Regulation Crime & Punishment Drug Policy Oversight & Reform Stem Cell Research Trade & Globalization	***Must-Have Issues*** Civil Rights Energy Policy Family Values Foreign Policy Jobs & Unemployment Welfare & Poverty

STATED ISSUE IMPORTANCE

The outcome is a visual tool that helps political strategists prioritize their efforts. For instance, "Key Drivers" are essential factors that must be addressed to sustain voter satisfaction, while "Constituent Unmet Needs" highlight areas that can distinguish the candidate and rally the voter base. "Must Haves" are issues that don't propel the campaign forward but can cause harm if neglected. "Indifference Points," though still relevant, generally reflect deeply held political views and don't influence election strategy.

Example 2 – Competitive Issue Targeting with Matrix Analysis

Matrix analysis in competitive issue targeting for political research involves mapping key issues across voter segments to identify areas of strategic opportunity. By creating a matrix with issues on one axis and demographic or psychographic voter groups on the other, researchers can evaluate the salience, alignment, and potential impact of each issue. This approach helps identify "winning issues"—those that resonate strongly with target voter segments and differentiate the campaign from opponents.

For example, a campaign may discover that climate action scores high among suburban swing voters but is underutilized by competitors, offering a chance to craft targeted messaging. The matrix enables prioritization of resources, ensuring the focus is on issues that maximize voter mobilization and persuasion within specific constituencies.

Our competitive issue targeting analysis goes beyond simply mapping candidate strengths in a quadrant. It incorporates a correlation column—a third dimension—to measure how strongly each issue aligns with the likelihood of an eventual vote, emphasizing the importance of highly correlated issues.

Figure 2 provides a visual representation of the three-dimensional matrix.

Figure 2 – Three-Dimensional Competitive Issue Targeting

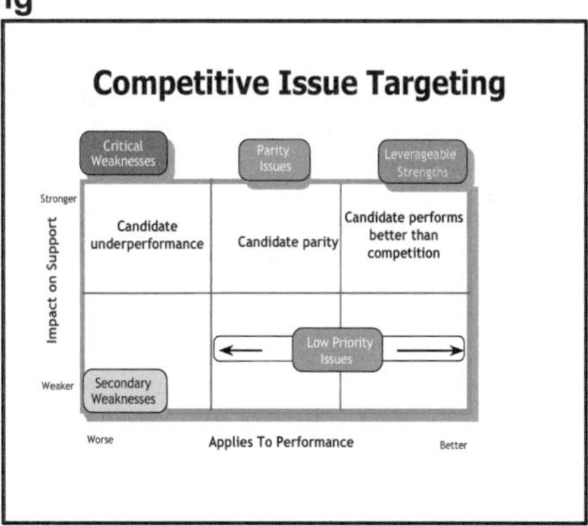

The results are illustrated in Table 1.

Table 1 – Three-Dimensional Competitive Issue Targeting – Harris vs. Trump

Total Attributes	Correlation of Intent to Vote With 'Describes Harris'	Top 3 Box (9 10 11) Percentages 'Describes Harris'	Top 3 Box (9 10 11) Percentages 'Describes Trump'	% Def Diff	STAT Difference	Vote Driver Class	Versus Opponent	IMP Rank
Is a strong leader	0.391	43%	55%	-12%	0.00	High	Weakness vs. Trump	1
Has the toughness to be President	0.370	41%	60%	-19%	0.00	High	Weakness vs. Trump	2
Has new ideas and a fresh approach to problems	0.368	50%	36%	13%	0.00	High	Strength vs. Trump	3
Would be steady in a crisis	0.353	39%	57%	-18%	0.00	High	Weakness vs. Trump	4
Would unite the country	0.341	32%	23%	9%	0.01	High	Strength vs. Trump	5
Has the right kind of experience to be President.	0.306	16%	53%	-37%	0.00	High	Weakness vs. Trump	6
Is a straight-talker, doesn't just say what people want to hear	0.302	47%	37%	11%	0.00	High	Strength vs. Trump	7
Can overcome the partisan politics in Washington	0.273	26%	27%	-2%	0.61	Low	Low Priority-Left	9
Will stand up to lobbyists and special interests	0.267	39%	33%	6%	0.12	Low	Low Priority-Left	10
Would change business as usual in Washington	0.258	37%	29%	8%	0.02	Low	Low Priority-Right	11
Would restore respect for America around the world	0.254	41%	50%	-9%	0.01	Low	Secondary Attribute	12
Would stand up for the middle class	0.199	50%	50%	0%	0.89	Low	Low Priority-Left	13
Will be tough on terrorists	0.186	37%	49%	-12%	0.00	Low	Secondary Attribute	14

Examining Table 1, it's evident where Trump holds perceived advantages over his opponent, while Harris also demonstrates notable strengths.

The issues are organized based on the first column, which indicates the importance of each attribute. This arrangement allows for a clear, three-dimensional visualization of actionable insights, all within a single table. By prioritizing attributes according to their significance, the table enables a more structured and efficient analysis.

This approach not only highlights key factors but also facilitates decision-making by providing a comprehensive view of the data in an easily interpretable format. The resulting visualization makes it simpler to identify patterns, relationships, and areas that require attention, all within one cohesive framework.

Ethical Breaches - Public Misconduct - Corruption Allegations: A Strategic Roadmap for Reputation Restoration and Management

Benjamin Franklin once said, “Glass, china, and reputations are easily cracked and never well mended.” In a global economy, 24/7 news cycle, and ubiquitous social media culture, reputations in the 21st century are as fragile as glass and china was in the 1700s. Corporations, brands, and people that recover from fractured reputations are those that recognize the importance of transparency and getting in front of the narrative when a scandal occurs.

Every reputation crisis is unique, shaped by the specific circumstances and the individuals or organizations involved. Some crises stem from large-scale product recalls, such as Merck’s Vioxx drug withdrawal, Toyota’s faulty gas pedal issues, Chipotle’s E. coli outbreaks, or Samsung’s Galaxy Note 7 recall, infamous for phones that caught fire.

Others emerge from data breaches or celebrity scandals. In 2024, Boeing continued to face heightened scrutiny over the quality and safety of its aircraft manufacturing. The Alaska Airlines door plug incident and subsequent investigations intensified concerns about Boeing’s production processes, quality control, and overall safety culture.

Political reputation scandals are equally prevalent. The frequency of personal political crises often correlates with an individual’s public profile and involvement in politics. For high-profile politicians, public figures, or strategists, crises can arise regularly due to intense media attention, the rapid pace of political developments, or deliberate opposition strategies.

For example:

Jack Abramoff Lobbying Scandal (2005): Lobbyist Jack Abramoff was convicted of fraud, tax evasion, and conspiracy to bribe public officials, Indian casinos, leading to the conviction of several politicians and aides. After a guilty plea Jack Abramoff was sentenced to six years in federal prison for mail fraud, conspiracy to bribe public officials, and tax evasion. He served 43 months before being released on December 3, 2010.

Rod Blagojevich Corruption Scandal (2008): Illinois Governor Rod Blagojevich was arrested and later impeached for attempting to sell the U.S. Senate seat vacated by President-elect Barack Obama. Blagojevich was sentenced to 14 years in federal prison in December 2011 after being convicted on 18 counts of corruption. Blagojevich served nearly 8 years of his 14-year sentence in a federal prison. On February 18, 2020, President Trump commuted Blagojevich's sentence, allowing him to be released from prison.

Flint Water Crisis (2014): Government officials in Flint, Michigan, were implicated in decisions that led to lead-contaminated drinking water, resulting in a public health crisis and widespread criticism of regulatory failures. The Flint Water Crisis led to extensive legal, civil, and criminal consequences due to the systemic failures and decisions that exposed residents to lead-contaminated water. In 2021, a $626 million settlement was reached, primarily funded by the State of Michigan, to compensate Flint residents for harm caused by lead exposure and other damages.

George Santos Fabricated Background (2022): Representative George Santos was found to have fabricated significant portions of his personal and professional background during his congressional campaign, leading to investigations and calls for his resignation. In May 2023 - Santos is arrested for 23 federal charges, including fraud and money laundering relating to campaign funds. In August 2024 Santos pleads guilty to felony charges in court. At the time of this writing, he is awaiting sentencing.

Senator Bob Menendez Corruption Charges (2024): Senator Menendez was convicted on multiple counts, including accepting bribes and acting as an illegal foreign agent, adding to a series of corruption cases involving New Jersey politicians. In July 2024 a jury convicted Senator Robert Menendez of corruption offenses. He was sentenced to eleven years in federal prison.

Reputation Survival and Comebacks
Prominent politicians often survive scandals through resilience and strategic recovery. Figures like Bill Clinton and Boris Johnson faced intense scrutiny yet retained influence. Skillful communication, public relations, and policy successes shift focus from controversies.

Below are some of the more historical political comebacks.

Bill Clinton (USA): Impeached for perjury and obstruction of justice related to his affair with Monica Lewinsky. Acquitted by the Senate, he completed his presidency and later became a prominent global diplomat and advocate for various causes.

Donald Trump (USA): Impeached twice during his first term—first for abuse of power and obstruction of Congress, and later for incitement of insurrection—he faced allegations of Russian interference, financial improprieties, and more. Despite the controversies, he was re-elected in 2024.

Silvio Berlusconi (Italy): The multi-term Prime Minister faced numerous corruption charges, tax fraud allegations, and sex scandals (notably the "Bunga Bunga" parties). Despite these, he remained a dominant figure in Italian politics for decades.

Benjamin Netanyahu (Israel): The long-serving Prime Minister has faced multiple corruption investigations and indictments but has continually returned to power, cementing his status as a pivotal figure in Israeli politics.

Marion Barry (USA): The former Mayor of Washington, D.C., was caught on video using crack cocaine and served time in prison. Remarkably, he was later re-elected to the city council and even returned as mayor, symbolizing an extraordinary political comeback.

François Mitterrand (France): During his presidency, he secretly maintained a second family, a fact revealed after his death. The controversy did little to tarnish his overall legacy as one of France's longest-serving leaders.

Angela Merkel (Germany): Faced challenges such as controversies over data privacy, yet her steady leadership ensured her long tenure as Chancellor, during which she became one of the world's most respected leaders.

Emmanuel Macron (France): Weathered controversies like the Benalla affair involving his security chief and widespread protests during his tenure. Despite these challenges, he secured re-election and continued to shape France's political landscape.

Effective reputation management requires a multi-tiered response. In this chapter, we are going to focus on the research aspect of a reputation management response, stopping short of full media strategy and follow-up investigations.

Crisis Erupts

Reputation management is, in many ways, like a political campaign. They are all unique. In politics, the office, the candidates, the constituencies, and the issues are different.

Governor Alex Carter faces a political reputation crisis after leaked documents reveal alleged misuse of public funds for personal expenses, including luxury vacations, home renovations, and an affair with a 19-year-old au pair.

The scandal, dubbed "Lavishgate," gains traction when a whistleblower provides detailed evidence, including posted nude photos of the au pair, now 26, and the possible love child who is just beginning kindergarten. Public outrage escalates as social media floods with hashtags like #ResignCarter. Opposition leaders demand an independent investigation, while Carter denies wrongdoing, claiming political sabotage.

Meanwhile, trusted allies distance themselves, fearing backlash. Public trust in Carter's administration plummets, sparking protests and calls for impeachment. The crisis highlights the fragility of political reputations in the digital age and the power of transparency.

The Carter team's consulting and media division urgently contacts the research team with a critical task: rehabilitate the governor's public image. They emphasize that there is a two-year window before the Republican primary. In Carter's state, the GOP primary effectively determines the election outcome, given that Republicans outnumber Democrats by a ratio of over 3-to-1 statewide, and independents in the state lean more conservative than the national average.

The top priority is to launch a study immediately, ideally before "Lavishgate" gains too much traction in the media. This study aims to identify key positive attributes associated with the governor—what we often refer to as "personal brand equity."

Every public personality has a personal brand. The goal of this initial phase of research is to get a baseline of the client's strongest personality equity—the one likely to survive the reputation – and the potential initial damage to that attribute.

Table 1 – Regression Analysis of Governor Carter's Favorability Ratings vs. Essential State Initiatives

Ratings: Governor Carter's Agenda Regarding These Essential State Issues	Standardized Beta
Invests in prevention, treatment, and recovery programs to address opioid addiction, especially in areas with high rates of abuse	0.9
Prioritizes the repair and modernization of roads, bridges, and public transit systems across the state	0.7
Develop comprehensive strategies to prevent flooding and manage State's rivers and water resources sustainably	0.7
Strengthens healthcare infrastructure in underserved areas, including mobile clinics and telehealth options	0.7
Ensures that all public schools, urban and rural alike, receive fair and adequate funding to reduce disparities in educational outcomes	0.6
Implements programs to attract businesses and create jobs in rural State through tax incentives and infrastructure development	0.5
Partners with local governments and developers to create affordable housing options for low- and middle-income families	0.4
Supports measures that protect religious expression in public spaces and allow religious organizations to operate without government interference	0.4
Supports the expansion of high-speed internet access to rural and underserved communities to enhance connectivity and economic opportunity	0.4
Increases scholarships and reduce tuition costs for State residents attending state colleges and universities	0.3
Supports the Second Amendment and push for laws that protect the right to bear arms, including opposing restrictive gun control measures.	0.3
Supports legislation that bans abortion at 6 weeks in the state	0.3
Offer training programs for displaced workers to gain skills in growing industries like technology, healthcare, and renewable energy	0.3
Supports the use of school vouchers funded by the state government as a way to empower parents with the freedom to choose the best educational environment for their children.	0.3
Expands support for State farmers with access to advanced technology, sustainable practices, and robust markets for their products	0.3
Increase funding and initiatives to protect State's state parks, forests, and recreational areas	0.1
Dependent Variable: Favorability Measure - Governor Alex Carter	

In Table 1, the key drivers of Governor Carter's favorability which are statistically significant, are highlighted in gray. A quick review of the regression reveals that Governor Carter is perceived more as a practical leader than a conservative firebrand. His focus on addressing drug addiction, healthcare, and state infrastructure appears to be the primary factors influencing his favorability. In contrast, conservative cultural issues like abortion, gun rights, and the use of state vouchers for private schools do not show statistical significance.

Step 1

Launch ads highlighting the governor's efforts to combat the opioid epidemic, along with a separate ad featuring footage of him overseeing the opening of a new highway or a major bridge repair. Additionally, run an ad emphasizing Governor Carter's initiatives to improve the state's ailing healthcare system.

Crisis Research Playbook

The crisis research playbook must incorporate hypothetical scenarios that may arise during the reputation phase. Respondents will be asked to share their perceptions and attitudes toward Carter, other statewide officeholders, and well-known personalities. The study will also gather insights on key lawmaker attributes, tracking shifts in these perceptions over time. It is important to monitor which attributes see increases or declines and determine which characteristics help sustain the candidate’s strength.

This will allow for a comprehensive analysis of public sentiment and how various factors influence the ongoing perception of the candidate and their standing in the political landscape.

As the scandal unfolds, treat the response like a political campaign war room. A strategic plan and rapid response team must be in place. One person takes charge, and clear roles—defining what each team member should and should not do—are developed and assigned. The lead reputation campaign manager is responsible for enforcing these roles. Typically, the key players include the following:

- C-suite, general counsel, and/or outside legal counsel
- Reputation communication counsel for strategy and message development
- Pollster/opinion research, analytics translator
- Strategic marketing/communications director

Once the team is established, a follow-up study typically evaluates messaging concepts and identifies effective messengers. Key questions include: How robust are the personal brand equities? Who emerges as the most credible and engaging messenger? (For example, could the governor's spouse be a viable option?)

Monitoring social media sentiment becomes crucial, utilizing tools like social network analysis to track discussions and gauge public buzz on platforms such as Twitter, TikTok, and Facebook. This real-time feedback provides valuable insights into public sentiment, highlighting which messages resonate. It allows the reputation management team to refine their strategy and maintain control of the narrative.

Gather data over a defined period to transform the brand conversation into a cohesive narrative rather than a static snapshot. As the scandal progresses and the Carter response evolves, the trajectory of the governor's political standing will become evident. This position will either stabilize, deteriorate, or strengthen depending on the effectiveness of the response and the public's perception.

Analyzing this data in real-time allows for strategic adjustments, ensuring the narrative aligns with the intended outcomes while mitigating potential risks. Such a focused approach enables a clear understanding of how the situation impacts the governor's reputation and overall political trajectory.

Unexpected issues will arise that demand answers, potentially impacting corporate reputation and the brand. Ongoing measurement of the personal brand, along with tracking and reputation studies, will provide valuable insights. Some key deliverables include the following:

- Carter personal brand perception
- Voter propensity measures
- Understand how bad the scandal could get
- Reach of the negative message to understand the real threat

Following the Monica Lewinsky scandal, President Bill Clinton embarked on a determined effort to rehabilitate his political career. Initially, the scandal severely tarnished his reputation, leading to impeachment proceedings in 1998. However, Clinton used several strategies to regain public trust and restore his political standing.

One key approach was his direct address to the public. Clinton publicly admitted to his misconduct and issued a formal apology, acknowledging his mistakes but maintaining that he did not commit perjury or obstruct justice. This apology, delivered in a televised address, helped to humanize him and rebuild his connection with voters.

Clinton also capitalized on his accomplishments during his presidency, including the strong economic growth, low unemployment rates, and welfare reform, to shift the focus away from the scandal. He emphasized these successes in speeches and public appearances, framing them as part of his legacy.

Figure 1 – Stages of Crisis Management

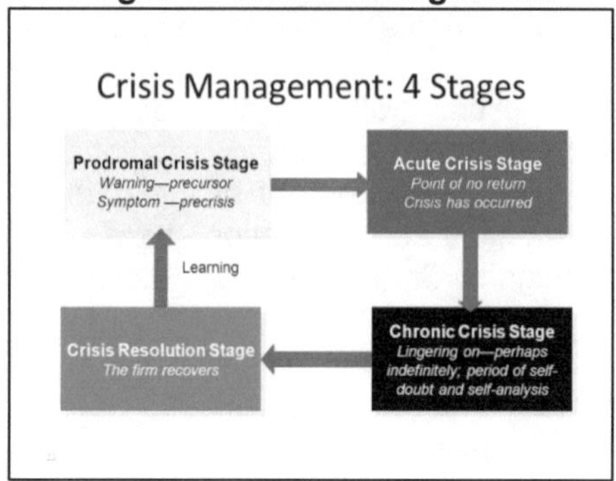

When a politician is facing scandal, key factors that need to be considered are the target audience, the type of scandal the organization is facing, and the stage in the scandal's life-cycle the scandal is in.

This framework provides the embattled party with a structured approach to assess their situation during the onset of a crisis ("as the storm breaks") and in the subsequent phases that follow.

Figure 2 - Elements of a Reputation Management Questionnaire

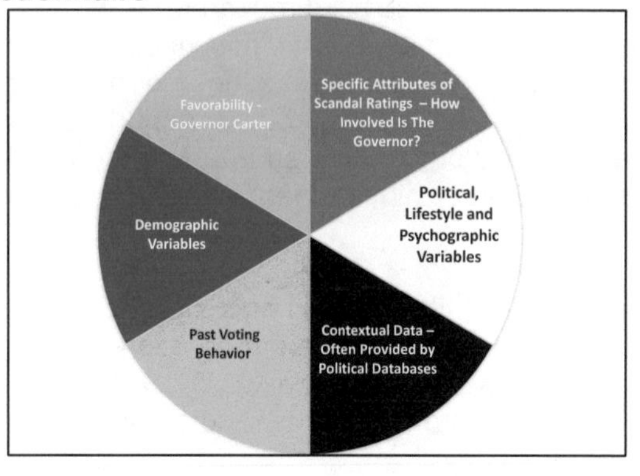

After gathering data we run an initial regression to see which accusations are sticking to Governor Carter.

This construction should have the following sequence in the survey.

- Pre-Array Favorability Ratings – On a 1-to-5 scale, how do you view Governor Alex Carter? *1=Not all Favorable, 5= Very Favorable*
- Allegations of Misconduct – On a 1-to-5 scale, please rate how much you think this applies to the governor? (Note: Carter's name should not appear in the array text. Rather he should be referred to as 'the Governor') *1=Not at all, 5= Very Much*
- Post-Array Favorability Follow-up –Again, on a 1-to-5 scale, how do you view Governor Alex Carter? *1=Not all Favorable, 5= Very Favorable*

For the next regression the dependent variable is (Post Array Favorability-Pre-Array Favorability). The new variable should be coded, 1=Negative or lower Favorability, 0=Favorability Unchanged or Improved. Allegation variables should also coded 1/0. I usually uses top box (4 5=1), (3 2 1=0). Results are shown in Table 2.

Table 2 – Regression Analysis of Governor Carter's Favorability Ratings vs. Essential State Initiatives

Allegations of Misconduct Against Governor Carter	Standardized Beta
Conflict of Interest – The governor exploited his governmental position for personal benefit	1.0
Fraud - The governor was accused of misusing a veterans' charity donor list to fund his political campaign, breaching campaign finance laws	0.9
Theft – The governor is accused of illegally taking public funds to pay for private expenses like vacations or home renovations	0.8
Abuse of Office – The governor faces allegations of using his position to authorize or overlook the misuse of public funds for personal benefit, including expenditures for personal matters	0.6
Misuse of State Resources – The governor is charged with using public resources for personal gain, including leveraging his position for personal publicity	0.4
Unwanted Sexual Advances - The governor has been accused of making unwanted sexual advances toward a young au pair responsible for caring for his children.	0.3
Violating Public Trust – The governor is accused of betraying the public's trust through personal misconduct during his time in office	0.2
Coercion or Intimidation – Forcing or pressuring someone into engaging in sexual activity against their will or under duress	0.2
Money Laundering – Hiding the origins of illicit funds by routing personal expenses through government accounts or using public resources to obscure wealth sources	0.1
Embezzlement – The governor is said to have misappropriated public funds for personal purposes, including diverting government money to fund luxury vacations or home renovations	0.1
Obstruction of Justice – The governor is accused of attempting to impede an investigation into blackmail claims, including falsifying information related to a compromising photo	0.1
Dependent Variable: Negative Change of Favorability Measure - Governor Alex Carter	

The bad news for Governor Carter is that allegations of financial improprieties appear to be negatively impacting his favorability. These significant claims focus on accusations of misusing his office for personal gain.

However, other accusations, including inappropriate sexual conduct and serious felonies such as money laundering, embezzlement, and obstruction of justice, have had no measurable statistical effect on his favorability ratings. Governor Carter still maintains the 'pragmatic conservative' label. In follow up questions, '"Invests in prevention to address opioid crisis" and "Develops comprehensive strategies to prevent flooding", and "Creates jobs in the overwhelming rural state" are still testing strongly for the governor. Lead with those messages while counteracting the negatives.

Insights for the Strategy Team
At this point the governor's public relations, media strategy, and advertising teams take over. I would point out the following:

Hold a Press Conference
- Address the public directly
- Issue a strong public denial (if appropriate)
- Reframe the allegations
- Highlight past integrity

Goals of the Crisis War Room
- Mobilize support from trusted allies
- Refocus public attention on achievements
- Leverage social media for transparency
- Hold town halls or public forums
- Stay focused on governance

Emphasize the new way forward and repeat immediate gubernational actions, such as:
- Providing transparent financial records
- Cooperating fully with investigations
- Announcing new policies to enhance financial accountability

In the next poll following the reputation tracker, it is crucial to test various messages and gather data within a defined time frame. During this phase, Governor Carter would like to highlight personal equities that have consistently reflected favorably on his administration. These include attributes such as pragmatism and statewide improvements in health and road infrastructure. If these attributes do not show an increase in favorability, they should be prioritized on the media team's agenda.

Benjamin Franklin recognized the critical value of reputation and the significant effort needed to repair a damaged one. Leveraging research-based consumer insights alongside timely and strategic communication proves to be a powerful approach for safeguarding and enhancing both personal and consumer brand equity.

Cross-Applying Consumer Strategies to Political Polling: Issue Effect Analysis

Issue Effect Analysis (IEA) is a visual, non-multivariate tool designed to identify which political positions, whether skewed too far left or right, are reducing a candidate's support. This method adapts analytical approaches typically used in adjacent research fields to the political landscape. In essence, Issue Effect Analysis is the political counterpart to the widely utilized 'Just About Right' (JAR) analysis, employed in industries such as consumer package goods, food and beverage, cosmetics, household products, pharmaceuticals, pet food, and consumer electronics. IEA provides a more nuanced understanding of how well a candidate's positions align with voter preferences and can rapidly pinpoint weaknesses in their platform or those of their opponents.

For background, a 'Just About Right' (JAR) analysis for consumer-packaged goods (CPG) is a sensory evaluation technique used to determine whether a product's specific attributes—such as sweetness, saltiness, or texture—fall within consumers' ideal range. The JAR scale typically consists of three categories: 'too little,' 'just about right,' and 'too much.' This method helps companies assess how well their product aligns with consumer preferences for each attribute, enabling them to optimize the product, identify weaknesses, and allow for side-by-side comparisons with multiple products.

Structure of the Survey and IEA Visuals

In political polling, the issue effect approach is used to evaluate voters' perceptions of candidates, policies, or campaign strategies by placing opinions on a spectrum from too extreme to moderate or balanced. Instead of relying on binary choices like "approve" or "disapprove," IEA polling asks respondents to determine whether a candidate's stance or a political position is "too liberal," "too conservative," or "agree with candidate position."

In order to run an Issue Effect Analysis, the survey has to be written with certain specific questions. The first is the *measurement variable*. The analysis must contain an 'Intend to Vote' or 'Favorability' rating of for our congressional candidate, Julieta Carrillo:
On a scale of 1-to-10, how likely are you to vote for Julieta Carrillo?

Next, the candidate is rated on a number of issues. The following are examples:

- On the following issues, please rate Julieta Carrillo:
  - Ensuring everyone has access to affordable health care
  - Protecting the little man and middle class
  - Protecting the environment
  - Immigration amnesty
  - Abortion rights
  - Native American rights
  - Seniors' issues
  - Keep government spending down.

Is Julieta Carrillo:

1. *Too conservative*
2. *Agree with her position*
3. *Too progressive*[5]

[5] This question can vary in complexity, but for clarity, we are presenting the simplest version. A five-point scale, often including options like "Somewhat too progressive" or "Somewhat too conservative," is also commonly used.

Table 1 – Issue Effect Map – Julieta Carrilloz

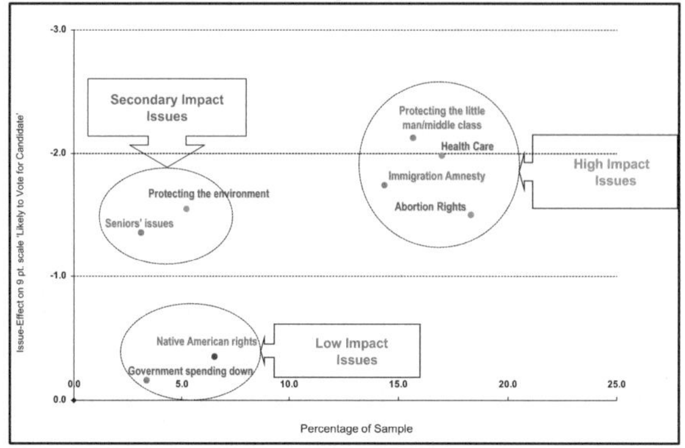

In the visual, a blue issue label indicates that Julieta Carrillo is too progressive on that particular issue, while a red label suggests that she is too conservative. The interpretation of an issue's position on the graph in the Issue Effect Analysis visual is outlined in detail in Table 2 (below).

Table 2 – Interpretation of the IAE Visual

- **Issue-Effect Measures the Loss of Support** – We measure the mean of 'Likely to Vote for Candidate' if the respondent thinks the candidate is either too right or left- leaning on an issue vs. 'Agree with candidate'.
  - **Y-axis:** Difference in mean from 'Too progressive/too conservative' and 'Likely to Vote for Candidate'.
  - **X-axis:** Percentage of voters who think Candidate is 'Too progressive/right-of-center'.
- **Chart Interpretation:**
  - **Top Right:** High Impact Issues. Strong opposition to the Candidate's position among a relatively high percentage of voters (above 10%).
  - **Top Left:** Secondary Impact Issues. High loss of support among a low percentage of voters.
  - **Bottom Left:** Low Impact Issues. A small percentage of voters with negligible influence on the candidate's support.

Insights from the IEA Analysis

The ability to interpret the IEA visual is crucial. Equally important is the next step: extracting the key insights relevant to the Carillo campaign, which are presented below.

High Impact Issues

Health Care: About 17% of respondents feel that Julieta Carrillo's stance is too progressive, leading to approximately a 2-point decrease in support from these voters compared to those who agree with her on this issue.

Protecting the Little Man and Middle Class: Around 15% of respondents believe the candidate's position is too conservative. These voters are more than 2 points less likely to support her compared to those who align with her views.

Abortion Rights: Roughly 18% of respondents find Julieta Carrillo's position too progressive, resulting in a 1.5-point drop in support.

Immigration Amnesty: Approximately 14% of respondents feel the candidate's stance is too conservative, leading to a 1.7-point decrease in their likelihood to vote for her compared to those who agree with her position.

Secondary Impact Issues

Protecting the Environment: Although Julieta Carrillo loses 1.5 points in support from voters who believe she is too progressive on this issue, only around 5% of respondents share this view.

Senior Issues: While the candidate loses 1.2 points among voters who feel she is too conservative on senior issues, this group represents just 4% of the respondents.

Low Impact Issues
These issues lack sufficient support from respondents and have too little influence for the Carrillo campaign to classify them as 'swing' issues.

In conclusion, cross-applying consumer strategies to political polling provides a powerful framework for understanding voter behavior and preferences. By using methods like segmentation and preference analysis, campaigns can better identify key issues, optimize their messaging, and assess how various political positions resonate with different voter groups. Techniques such as the "Just About Right" (JAR) analysis, widely used in consumer industries, can be adapted to the political arena to evaluate where a candidate's stance may be too extreme or too moderate, offering a nuanced view of voter sentiment.

This approach not only refines how campaigns target and persuade voters but also highlights potential weaknesses in a candidate's platform. Much like companies use consumer data to improve products and align with market needs, political campaigns can utilize these strategies to adapt and fine-tune their policies and messaging. Ultimately, integrating consumer strategies into political polling allows for more precise and actionable insights, improving a campaign's ability to connect with voters and win their support.

Voter Predictive Modeling – Optimizing Communications Impact and Message Reach
It's all about positive eyeballs per dollar spent.

Imagine you have a database of, say, ten million voters, consumers, or perhaps one hundred thousand association members. This database is packed with detailed information. Beyond the usual data like demographics (gender, age, income, etc.) and political details (party affiliation, donations, voting history in primaries and general elections), it holds a wealth of other personal insights.

For instance, it includes whether the individual rents or owns their home, the number of private schools in their area, whether there's a working woman in the household, how many children live in the home, and if they own a DVD player or support health or environmental causes. It also tracks if they own an SUV, subscribe to magazines, and much more.

With an election approaching, your organization wants to reach swing voters or rally those who may support your key issue. To do this, you're planning to send direct mail or make phone calls to these potential supporters—something that will inspire or persuade them.

Similarly, a credit card company may want to send promotional samples to a million households but hopes to minimize the chances of people discarding them without a second thought. The goal is to make sure the message resonates and grabs attention.

Imagine you're trying to reach swing voters in the Pennsylvania—a critical swing state where conditions are far from ideal. Based on existing records, you estimate that around 20% of your audience are likely swing voters. You could send a flyer to all ten million people, knowing that only one in five would be a potential hit. However, a more effective approach would be to target just the swing voters, improving efficiency and reducing costs. The challenge? You don't yet know exactly who they are.

So you can't actually target them. But you can build a model and make a *very educated guess.*

In addition to your primary database, you have around ten thousand records where you've identified your target group.

These records might come from other lists, primary research with ID numbers that can be traced back to your main database, or even company databases. These records allow you to establish a connection between 'swing' voters and key characteristics that help define them. Virtual targeting takes this data further by building and testing a profile of who your target audience really is.

What is Virtual Targeting

What sets our target group, swing voters, apart from non-swing voters? Are there specific traits we can use to identify and understand their perspectives? How can we combine various individual attributes to make a single assessment of the likelihood that someone is a 'swing' voter?

Virtual targeting addresses these questions through a combination of statistical techniques that: 1) identifies key characteristics distinguishing the target group, and 2) constructs a linear equation to apply to each of the ten million records, generating a 'score' for each individual. By sorting these scores, the goal is to identify the group with the highest scores, which are most likely to include the swing voters.

Step One

The first step is to analyze the wide range of variables available and, using the known swing voters, identify which factors differentiate our target group from non-targets.

Two key techniques can be used: regression analysis and CHAID, a chi-square method that generates a decision tree. The variables at the top of the tree are the most effective at distinguishing between swing and non-swing voters, while their importance decreases further down the branches. However, any variable that appears in the top five or six branches is a strong candidate for inclusion in the final model.

A detailed explanation of regression and CHAID analysis goes beyond the scope of this article. In essence, both methods aim to identify a key variable—a measure of association—between our target group and the characteristics present across hundreds of variables in the dataset. These analyses help eliminate insignificant variables when examining voting profiles. The variables deemed significant are then recoded to reduce model error.

Below is an example to the recoding scheme for our Pennsylvania project.

Figure 1 – Variables from the Political Database That are Significantly Related to Voting Behavior

Significant Demographic or Behavioral Variables	Recode
Party registration	1=GOP, 2=Democratic, 3=Independent
Contribution to environmental group	1=Yes, 0=No
Working women in household	1=Yes, 0=No
Unemployment rate in Pennsylvania	3=Full time, 2=Part time, 1=Student, 0=Unemployed
Primary 2020	1=Voted, 0=Did not vote
Attend religious services regularly	1=Yes, 0=No
Married	1=Married, 0=Not married
Subscribed to one or more magazines or publications	1=Yes, 0=No
Bank credit card	1=Use bank credit card regularly, 0=No, do no use bank credit card regularly
High private school attendance district	1=Yes, children attend private school, 0=No children in private school
Age	Under 40=3 41-65=2 65+=1
Household party	, 2=Mixed, 1=Republican, 3=Democrat, 0=No affiliation
General election 2020	1=Voted, 0=Did not vote
General election 2022	1=Voted, 0=Did not vote
Primary election 2022	1=Voted, 0=Did not vote

As expected, several political variables, such as voting frequency and party affiliation, have made it into the model. This is logical since we are targeting a potentially politically neutral group of voters. Naturally, those who are not politically neutral—such as regular primary voters—stand out as key distinguishing variables.

Surprisingly, several less obvious demographic and social factors also made it into the model. For instance, if a person is married, resides in a district with high private school enrollment, and holds a bank credit card, their likelihood of being a swing voter becomes easier to pinpoint.

Step Two

Now we know what should be place into the model. Either the initial regressions or CHAID trees have told us. The next step is to run the model.

There are several multivariate techniques that can be applied for this purpose, with names like logistic regression or forecasting membership using an exponential probability model.

These methods are effective in the right scenarios and often sound sophisticated enough to impress clients, reassuring them that the model is complex and refined. In reality, many credit card companies use these techniques on their massive databases with great success.

However, Pennsylvania is a state that prefers straightforward, no-nonsense approaches. Our goal is to produce clear, actionable results that can easily be mapped back to the main list. That is the reason I have chosen to use discriminant analysis—a multivariate technique that evaluates our input variables and generates coefficients that measure how well each attribute distinguishes between swing voters and those who are firmly committed.

Discriminant analysis generates a "discriminant function," which is a linear equation where coefficients are applied to respondent attributes to produce a score. Based on this discriminant score, we calculate the likelihood of each group membership (i.e., swing voter status) by comparing it to what we know about swing voters from the smaller sample. In simple terms, the respondent's attributes are entered, producing a score, which is then matched against a chart to determine the likelihood of them being a swing voter.

As with any advanced statistical analysis, the process generates a flood of data. However, there are three key outputs we need to focus on: the beta scores of the discriminant function (referred to as the raw coefficients), the standardized coefficients (which highlight the most influential variables), and the discriminant score, along with the percentage likelihood that this score identifies someone as a member of our target group—swing voters.

The raw and standardized coefficients are used for both descriptive and classification purposes, which I will explain further below. The discriminant score, once calculated, becomes the primary tool for classifying individuals in future assessments.

In the virtual targeting model, there is an additional measure we use that isn't typically part of discriminant analysis. This measure evaluates the model's effectiveness in identifying swing voters.

The method is simple: after running the analysis; the software assigns each respondent a score. We then sort the list from highest to lowest and examine the top 10%, for example.

The goal is to assess how much better this sorted list performs compared to a random sample.

For instance, with our Pennsylvania list, we expect 20% of voters to be swing voters. If, within the top 10% of our sorted list, 30% are identified as swing voters, we know our model is 50% more efficient than a random sample.

First Example
Standardized discriminant scores in a voter predictive model represent the contribution of each predictor variable (such as age, education, or party affiliation) to the discriminant function, which is designed to classify or predict voter behavior.

These scores are standardized to allow comparison across variables with different scales, highlighting their relative importance in distinguishing between predefined voter groups, such as likely voters versus non-voters or supporters of different candidates.

Figure 2 presents the sorted output of our discrimination model, with the important variables highlighted in gray. A negative coefficient indicates a negative discriminator, meaning these actions do not align with the dependent variable. These negative discriminators are just as significant as positive ones, as they reveal clearly which variables are the most non-descriptive for our target—swing voters.

Figure 2 – Standardized Discriminant Scores – Voter Predictive Model

Significant Demographic or Behavioral Variables	Standardized Discriminant Coefficients
Party registration, (1=Rep, 2=Dem, 3=Ind)	0.31
Contribution to Environmental Group	0.10
Working women in Household	0.10
Unemployment Rate in Pennsylvania	0.04
Primary 2002	0.00
Attend Religious Services Regularly	-0.05
Married 1=Married, 0=Other	-0.05
Subscribed to one or more magazines or publications, responded to a survey, or entered a sweepstakes within the past 2 years	-0.06
Bank credit card	-0.08
High Private school attendance district	-0.08
Age Under 40=3 41-65=2 65+=1	-0.08
Household party, 2=Mixed, 1=Republican, 3=Democrat, 0=No affiliation	-0.15
General Election 2020	-0.28
General Election 2022	-0.29
Primary Election 2022	-0.36

Not surprisingly the most discriminating factor is that the person is an independent. That is, not a member of either political party. The two other telling factors to determine swing is that the person contributes to a religious group and there is a working woman in the household.

Not surprisingly, if a person has voted in the primary election in 2022, or in a recent general election, he has a high negative coefficient. It is unlikely that he is a swing voter.

Virtual targeting serves both descriptive and predictive purposes. The descriptive aspect, as shown in Figure 2, reveals which factors are most (or least) significant when running the model, providing valuable insights. However, the true strength of this technique lies in its ability to predict a person's group membership. This predictive power is where the real value is found.

The chart below (Figure 3) illustrates how a given person receives a discriminant score. The raw coefficients (not standardized, as above) are multiplied by a respondent's answer, then tallied to create one 'score'.

Figure 3 – Calculation of Voter Predictive Model for One Respondent

Variables Present in Model Equation	Raw Discriminant Function Coefficients*	Coded Answer to Question	Sum of Raw Discriminant
Party registration, (1=Rep, 2=Dem, 3=Ind)	0.75	1	0.75
Contribution to Environmental Group	0.73	0	0.00
Working women in Household	0.63	1	0.63
Unemployment Rate in Pennsylvania	0.19	1	0.19
Primary 2002	0.16	3	0.47
Attend Religious Services Regularly	0.13	0	0.00
Married 1=Married, 0=Other	0.13	1	0.13
Subscribed to one or more magazines or publications, responded to a survey, or entered a sweepstakes within the past 2 years	0.12	7	0.83
Bank credit card	0.11	1	0.11
High Private school attendance district	0.00	1	0.00
Age Under 40=3 41-65=2 65+=1	0.00	1	0.00
Household party, 2=Mixed, 1=Republican, 3=Democrat, 0=No affiliation	-0.02	4	-0.06
General Election 2002	-0.04	3	-0.11
General Election 2000	-0.23	1	-0.23
Primary Election 2000	-0.36	2	-0.73
*Used to calculate discriminant score	Discriminant Score	1.9950	

At the bottom of Figure 3 this example's score has been calculated. It is 1.9950. So, is that good?

The final key output in our example is a list of all discriminant scores along with the probability that each respondent is a swing voter. This data can be sorted and presented in a table, a portion of which is shown below.

Figure 4 – Condensed Table of Raw Discriminant Scores and Likelihood of Swing Voter Status

Raw Score	Swing Probability
2.65	82%
2.64	80%
2.61	80%
2.59	79%
2.56	79%
2.37	76%
2.36	76%
2.36	76%
2.36	76%
2.36	76%
2.00	61%
2.00	61%
1.99	61%
1.99	61%
1.42	50%
1.42	50%
1.41	49%
1.41	49%
0.00	33%
0.00	33%
-0.01	33%
-0.01	33%

This table is quite extensive and serves as a 'look-up' reference. Once an individual's survey responses are scored, their total score can be compared to this table to determine the percentage likelihood of them being a swing voter. For example, a score of 1.9950 corresponds to a 60% chance of being a swing voter. Target him.

How Good is The Model?
The final and most crucial step: How effective is the model? Is it worth applying this scoring method to all ten million records?

Figure 5 – Ratio Percentile of Voters to Swing Percentage

% Total Sample	% Of Sample that is Swing Voters	Index (Base=20%)	% Better
0	0	0	0
10	41%	205	105
20	35%	175	75
30	31%	155	55
40	29%	145	45
50	27%	135	35
60	24%	118	18

To interpret the chart from left to right: After scoring the known swing voters and ranking them from highest to lowest, what percentage of the top 10% are actually swing voters?

The chart shows that 41% of the top 10% are swing voters (second column). In a random selection, we would expect only 20% to be swing voters. By dividing 41 by 20, we find a ratio of 2.05, indicating that the model more than doubles the efficiency of identifying swing voters. When this ratio is multiplied by 100, it yields an index score of 205, demonstrating exceptionally strong performance.

Examining the top 20% of the sorted sample, 35% are swing voters. This demonstrates that the model is 1.75 times more effective than random selection, yielding an index score of 175.

As we progress through the sample in descending order of scores, the efficiency naturally declines, as lower scores correspond to a reduced likelihood of an individual being a swing voter.

Here's the impact: if the organization sends one million mailings without using virtual targeting, it would likely reach around 200,000 swing voters. By contrast, employing virtual targeting and applying the model's scores to the general database could reach 410,000 swing voters with the same budget.

.

Accurately Polling Ranked Choice Races Using Statistical Inference – Maximum Difference Analysis

How does a pollster take a snapshot of a crowded, ranked choice voting primary three months from election day? It is not as simple as asking respondents who they are going to vote for, and who would be their second choice. The reason is that candidates may be knocked off the scorecard once the vote counting begins.

A ranked-choice voting system (RCV) is an electoral system in which voters rank candidates by preference on their ballots. If a candidate wins a majority of first-preference votes, he or she is declared the winner. If no candidate wins a majority of first-preference votes, the candidate with the fewest first-preference votes is eliminated. First-preference votes cast for the failed candidate are eliminated, lifting the second-preference choices indicated on those ballots. A new tally is conducted to determine whether any candidate has won a majority of the adjusted votes. The process is repeated until a candidate wins an outright majority.

This article will reveal a highly effective way to *rank-order* candidates at any given moment during the race. It relies not only on direct voting intentions, but takes into account second and further choices and candidates who do not have high name recognition. Moreover, this simple method can give can be tracked over time as the election nears and the race tightens to help form communication and electoral strategy.

Maximum Difference Scaling

Maximum Difference Analysis (or scaling) is another method of choice modeling. Essentially, Maximum Difference has the respondent specify the "best" and "worst" choices from a set of three or more objects, in our case candidates.

Maximum Difference allows the pollsters and political strategists to test a large number of candidates without having to resort to difficult manual ranking. It is more effective than the simple, 'Who would you vote for' approach and takes into account matchups among candidates that might not otherwise be directly compared. This methodology allows strategists to gauge positive sentiment, negative sentiment, and, most importantly, name recognition among the candidates. Most importantly, it lets the campaign team know 'what is going on' months before the race heats up.

Our Large Primary

For the sake of this article, let's use the top 8 current candidates to be mayor of a non-named city. Past election rules stated that if one candidate did not garner 40% of the vote, there would be a run-off.

Under the new rules, as stated above, if the first-choice candidate fails the count goes to the second-place candidate. This continues until one candidate tops the 50% mark. Given these new rules, there will certainly be a winner on primary day.

There are eight candidates. The election is three months away, so voters are not paying attention to the race yet. A congressman and former mayoral candidate are sucking up a lot of media attention, and several long-time and popular city figures are in the race as well.

Below is a list of fictional major candidates. At this point in the race, the clear winner of a straight poll is "Undecided" at 26%. The celebrity candidate comes in second with 16% - thus, the front runner. But the race is fluid.

Table 1 – List of Mayor Candidates and Qualifications

Candidate	Qualification
Kerrel Bennett	Banking Executive
Jadonna Moses	Female African-American Writer
Arthur Keegan	Former Obama Administration Official
Lonquille Wheeler	University Professor
Jacob Jacobs	Career-Long City Politician
Reuben Hall	Head of City Council
Susana Gálvez	Former Sanitation Commissioner
Carl Hu	Known Local Congressman and Past Mayoral Candidate

After demographics in the opening (or closing) of the poll, the respondent is asked, "Thinking about the candidates running in this year's Democratic primary election for mayor, if the election were held today, who would be your first-choice candidate?"

Then asked, 'If the Democratic mayoral primary were held today, who would be your second choice candidate?'

These responses give the same results as a straight poll, most likely. Below are the outputs of this first round of questions.

Table 2 – Outcome of Initial Poll First/Second and Top Two Percentages Combined

Candidate	First Place Percentage	Summary First/Second Choice
Reuben Hall	20%	35%
Carl Hu	19%	24%
Susana Gálvez	16%	25%
Jacob Jacobs	11%	16%
Jadonna Moses	5%	8%
Arthur Keegan	4%	7%
Kerrel Bennett	3%	5%
Lonquille Wheeler	2%	4%
Undecided	20%	26%

The race is still in flux. No candidate wins outright. There is no way to be sure (other than to ask) the likelihood of their second-place voting choice to be set.

What we are proposing is another "snapshot" of the race. One which could point to future movement of the polls once the race picks up steam. Additionally, our method factors in unfavorable feelings towards a candidate vis-à-vis other candidates and is a leading indicator of the effect of the second choice.

Maximum Difference Scaling in Use

Maximum Difference (MaxDiff) in a political context can be used to rank candidates a political race. This is the method we will use today to take a look at the city Mayoral Race example.

Here we are seeking in-the-moment voting preferences for candidates without asking for whom respondents will actually vote. The methodology also takes into account candidates with low-name recognition. In a MaxDiff construction, the respondent is shown a group of candidates and asked which is most likely to vote in the scenario, and which is least likely to vote for.

We will go through this exercise with each respondent. They will see a series of prompts that look like the following:

You will now be asked to rate candidates within sets of four. If you are not aware of a candidate, do not choose him/her, even if more than one unknown is shown in the choice scenario.

Of the four candidates below, at the moment who are MOST likely to vote for and the LEAST likely to vote for?

1) Lonquille Wheeler
2) Reuben Hall
3) Luciana Mireles
4) Jacob Jacobs

Of the four candidates below, at the moment who are MOST likely to vote for and the LEAST likely to vote for?

1) Reuben Hall
2) Luciana Mireles
3) Kerrel Bennett
4) Arthur Keegan

They are asked this four more times, with the candidates rotating in position and order. Each candidate will be seen three times. The rotations for the survey design will not remain the same for all respondents. That is, if we are polling 300 likely voters, we will generate 100 different splits—or order they see the candidates. This makes the outcome robust.

Output includes both a raw score and a choice coefficient, that is, the likelihood of a candidate being chosen if his name appears on a scenario (this is derived from logistic regression).

Another way to state this is as the Bayesian coefficient commonly used in most decision-choice models. We examine this measure first to determine the 'horse race' snapshot.

Each respondent receives a score for *each* candidate. If each score is recoded to be the rank of the eight candidates, then we are set up to view the data as it would be shown in a ranked choice vote.

- The first round shows the recoded variables for first choice.
- In the second round we eliminate the last place finisher, add first/second choice to the variable (to simulate second choices), and then retally.
- In the third round we eliminate the last place finisher, add first/second/third choice to the variable (to simulate second choices), and then retally.
- This process continues until one candidate passes the 50% threshold.
- The poll can be repeated weekly, monthly, semi-monthly, without being rewritten. Results can then be show as a time series to visual the shape of the race.

In the table below we are shown the results three months out of the primary.

With this result set, we can see that Reuben Hall might be the winner if people voted today in a simple primary. However, he has close competition from Susana Galvez. It is interesting that neither of the two front runners received many 2nd, 3rd, or 4th place votes. We can assume that the electorate is broken into camps regarding the two top candidates. Other serious candidates, like Jadonna Moses and Carl Hu are in the running strongly in the first rounds, but then fail to grow as the process continues.

Table 3 - City Primary Ranked Choice Primary Results

	Round 1	Round 2	Round 3	Round 4	Round 5	Round 6	Round 7
	%	%	%	%	%	%	%
Reuben Hall	25.5%	26.5%	28.1%	31.9%	35.4%	42.7%	51.1%
Susana Gálvez	24.0%	24.8%	28.1%	30.3%	34.0%	40.5%	48.9%
Jadonna Moses	15.9%	16.5%	18.1%	17.6%	17.0%	16.7%	Eliminated
Carl Hu	14.3%	14.8%	14.6%	14.1%	13.6%	Eliminated	
Jacob Jacobs	5.6%	5.8%	6.3%	6.1%	Eliminated		
Lonquille Wheeler	4.8%	5.0%	4.9%	Eliminated			
Kerrel Bennett	6.3%	6.5%	Eliminated				
Arthur Keegan	3.5%	Eliminated					

Below is the table for final results from the 2021 New York City mayoral primary. As you will note, the outputs look similar. There are differences. The New York primary had more candidates and rules eliminated more than one candidate per round. These can be built into any polling simulation.

Table 4 – New York City Ranked Primary Results - 2021

2021 New York City Mayoral Democratic Primary Election								
Candidate	Round 1	Round 2	Round 3	Round 4	Round 5	Round 6	Round 7	Round 8
	%	%	%	%	%	%	%	%
Eric Adams	30.7%	30.8%	30.8%	31.2%	31.7%	34.6%	40.5%	50.4%
Kathryn Garcia	19.6%	19.6%	19.6%	19.9%	20.5%	24.4%	30.5%	49.6%
Maya Wiley	21.4%	21.4%	21.4%	22.0%	22.4%	26.1%	29.1%	Eliminated
Andrew Yang	12.2%	12.2%	12.3%	12.6%	13.0%	14.8%	Eliminated	
Scott Stringer	5.5%	5.5%	5.5%	5.7%	6.1%	Eliminated		
Dianne Morales	2.8%	2.8%	2.8%	3.2%	3.3%			
Raymond McGuire	2.7%	2.7%	2.7%	2.8%	3.0%			
Shaun Donovan	2.5%	2.5%	2.5%	2.6%	Eliminated			
Aaron Foldenauer	0.8%	0.8%	0.8%	Eliminated				
Art Chang	0.7%	0.8%	0.8%					
Paperboy Prince	0.4%	0.4%	0.4%					
Joycelyn Taylor	0.3%	0.3%	0.3%					
Isaac Wright Jr.	0.2%	0.2%	Eliminated					
Write-ins	0.2%	Eliminated						

MaxDiff ranking is a sophisticated method to gauge a "snapshot" of a race in time. It measures distinct aspects of a political race. MaxDiff can be useful in a crowded primary, a scattered parliamentary election, or an open race with many candidates from all parties.

Traditional polling might be able to gauge the rivalry between the top tier candidates, but it is not able to determine if a candidate has a strong first round showing, but then falls off a cliff. Traditional polling would also miss if a dark horse candidate can surge in the 3rd or 4th round and emerge the winner.

There are many applications for the accurate measurement of choice modeling. MaxDiff ranking is not new, but is emerging as the simplest and most effective choice for political strategy. It can be used to assess the extendibility of a candidate's strength, to refine a campaign's communication efforts, and/or as a way of monitoring the competition. Whatever its application, this method of voter measurement is a sophisticated tool that helps keep strategists one step ahead.

Item Count Method – Estimating Voter Turnout Among Low Turnout Populations

The outcome of an election often depends on who shows up to vote on Election Day. Reliable turnout predictions are essential for making key strategic decisions, from shaping messages and outreach to planning advertising and get-out-the-vote efforts. To accurately forecast Election Day voting patterns, high-quality research and thoughtful analysis are crucial.

Yet, surveys often overestimate voter turnout. Why? Simply put, voters lie.

Political researchers have found that respondents often deliberately misrepresent their voting behavior to appear more responsible and socially desirable to the interviewer. This phenomenon is known as social desirability distortion, and it introduces bias into the data.

Estimating voting percentages among low-voting populations presents significant challenges due to a combination of underrepresentation, social desirability bias, and inconsistent voting patterns. These populations often include younger voters, lower-income groups, and minority communities, who may not be as reliably engaged in the electoral process.

Survey data can be skewed by respondents overstating their likelihood to vote, while traditional polling methods may fail to adequately capture these groups, leading to inaccurate turnout projections. Additionally, fluctuating levels of political engagement and barriers to voting, such as access issues or disillusionment, further complicate efforts to predict turnout within these populations, resulting in less precise estimates and potential misallocation of campaign resources.

In recent years, the Item Count Method has gained increasing popularity. This approach asks respondents to report only the number of behaviors they have engaged in from a provided list, without identifying which specific behaviors.

This article will provide a brief explanation of the Item Count Method and present a case study to demonstrate how to implement it in order to estimate voter turnout.

Item Count Method
The Item Count Method (ICM) is a survey technique designed to reduce social desirability bias, especially when asking about sensitive topics. Instead of directly asking respondents whether they've engaged in specific behaviors, the method provides a list of behaviors and asks respondents to indicate only the total number of behaviors they have engaged in—not which ones.

Here's how it works:

- **Control Group and Treatment Group**: Respondents are divided into two groups. The control group receives a list of non-sensitive behaviors, while the treatment group receives the same list with an additional sensitive behavior included.
- **Counting Responses**: Both groups are asked how many of the listed behaviors they have engaged in, without identifying any specific behavior.
- **Estimating Sensitive Behavior**: By comparing the average number of behaviors reported by the control and treatment groups, researchers can estimate the prevalence of the sensitive behavior in the population. The difference between the two averages is attributed to the sensitive item.

This method helps ensure privacy for respondents and can yield more honest responses for sensitive questions like illegal behavior, personal beliefs, or controversial activities.

Estimating Voter Turnout

In the following example, the researcher aims to estimate the percentage of eligible voters who participated in the last congressional election during a non-presidential year. This poll was conducted one year after the non-presidential election cycle.

One group was presented with a list of five items. Participants were informed that the questionnaire was designed to promote honest responses and were instructed not to indicate whether any specific item was true. Instead, they were asked to report how many of the five items applied to them.

How Many of the Following Have You Done in the Past Year?

Civic Behaviors - Group 1
Owned a gun
Went to see a movie in a threatre
Given money to a charitable organization
Written a letter to the editor
Volunteered for a local civic activity

While reporting how many items were true, participants never directly confirmed any specific item. For example, if someone answered "three," they were indicating that three out of the five items applied to them.

A second group of respondents received the same list, with one additional item—the behavior the researcher is interested in measuring.

How Many of the Following Have You Done in the Past Year?

Civic Behaviors - Group 2
Owned a gun
Went to see a movie in a threatre
Given money to a charitable organization
Written a letter to the editor
Volunteered for a local civic activity
Voted in your local congresssional election

By subtracting the average number of behaviors reported by the first group from the average reported by the second group, researchers can estimate the proportion of individuals in the second group who engaged in the behavior of interest.

When designing an Item Count Method experiment, there are several important guidelines to follow.

- The behavior used on the item count method list should be such that few respondents have performed all or none of them. Reporting only one activity negates the anonymity.
- Behaviors should be within the same 'category'. For example, if one is investigating risky sexual behavior, then other risky behaviors should be included on the list. It the goal is to estimate voter turnout, other civil activities should be included.
- A separate sample for direct reporting may be included for comparison.
- Larger samples enhance estimate stability and accuracy.

Below are preliminary results, by gender.

Table 1 – Prediction of Voting Behavior

	Total	Women	Men
Group 1	2.35	2.67	2.03
Group 2	2.72	3.08	2.36
Estimated Proportion of Congressional Off-Year Voting (Group 2 - Group 1)	0.37	0.41	0.33

The base rate estimate for the behavior of interest is calculated by subtracting the two group averages: mean (Group 2) - mean (Group 1). In this case, Group 1 reported an average of 2.35 behaviors, while Group 2 reported 2.72 behaviors.

Therefore, the estimated voter turnout in this population for the last federal election cycle is 2.72 - 2.35 = 0.37, meaning approximately 37% of this low-voting population turned out to vote in the previous non-presidential congressional election.

When broken down by gender, our sample shows that women have a slightly higher voting rate, which aligns with data from the Center for American Women and Politics at Rutgers University. Their reports indicate that in every presidential election since 1980, voter turnout rates for women have equaled or exceeded those of men.

The tendency of voters to lie when asked directly can be mitigated in research by using the indirect Item Count Method. This approach allows researchers to rely on a solid statistical foundation when making strategic decisions related to voter turnout.

In this way, the research data remains accurate, even when voters are not completely truthful.

Political Prediction - How Nate Silver Does It

Nate Silver beat them all. Joe Scarborough, the conservative host of "Morning Joe" on MSNBC, attacked Silver during the election. He apologized, sort of, acknowledging that Silver did get it right. Politico.com called him a “one-term” celebrity, saying, “For all the confidence Silver puts in his predictions, he often gives the impression of hedging.” (Later, Silver replied, “Politico covers politics like sports, but ‘not in an intelligent way at all.”)

Nate Silver, for those who don’t know, writes the FiveThirtyEight blog in the New York Times and is the best-selling author of *The Signal and the Noise*. In the book, Silver examines the world of prediction, investigating how we can distinguish a true signal from a universe of noisy data. It is about prediction, probability, and why most predictions fail—but not all.

What had folks attacking Silver was this: He predicted elections far more accurately than most pollsters and the noisy pundits on Politico, The Drudge Report, MSNBC and others. In his book, Silver described his model as “bringing Moneyball to politics.” That is, producing statistically-driven results.

Silver actually popularized the use of probabilistic models in predicting elections. Plainly stated, Silver produces the probability of a range of outcomes, rather than just who wins. When a candidate is at, say, a 90% chance of winning, Silver will call the race. What made Silver famous was his extremely accurate prediction of voter percentages. Pundits are almost always far off. However loath pollsters are to admit it, polls are almost always wrong, too. However, the average of polls is always more accurate. And a systematic probability model of the average of polls is almost always right. Think of it as political crowdsourcing.

Silver has built one of the best models out there. It's accurate, consistent, and totally statistical. One advantage of being totally statistical is that his model can be replicated. This piece will review the process, explaining how Silver built his model, what his results mean and how to use them going forward.

The Basics
To run Silver's model, here is what you will need
- Microsoft Excel
- A source of campaign finance and election data
- Historical data to set "polling weights"

The first step is to calculate the "poll weight," a measure of how much an individual poll counts when averaged with other polls. The poll weight consists of three values:
- **Recency**: The older a poll, the lower the accuracy. A recency factor is calculated using a relatively simple decay function. Think of a poll as having a shelf-life, as does a pharmaceutical product or package good. The longer on the shelf, the less potent the poll is.

- **Sample Size**: When shown on television, a poll might have a spread of +/- 4%. This spread is calculated using sample size. As a general rule, the larger the sample size, the more accurate the poll.

- **Pollster Rating**: Silver alludes to how his polling does this in a 2010 blog. He does not, however, completely reveal his secret sauce. Without going into too much statistical detail, Silver uses historical data and regression analysis to create an accuracy measure for pollsters. Better pollsters have positive ratings; worse have negative ratings.

After the information is created, the next step is to create a weighted polling average. That is, take the mean of each poll within the state using the three weights described above. For smaller races, like congressional or state races, polling data might be scarce, particularly in uncontested races. However, presidential contests, as we know, offer a deluge of data to be plugged in. Silver does not say exactly how he combines the weights. I multiply them and then weight the polls.

Error

A weighted polling average, like all averages, contains an error and a weighted mean—the weighted mean is the exact result, the *one* number that pops out of the calculation. Error is the average distance of each data point to the weighted mean. In creating a polling prediction, we utilize the error around the weighted mean. The smaller the average distance around the weighted mean, the error, the more accurate the poll.

When examining what Silver considers important in interpreting error (below), we get a good snapshot of what makes a poll accurate, and what makes a poll less accurate:

- Error is higher in races with fewer polls.
- Error is higher in races where the polls disagree with each other.
- Error is higher in races with a large number of undecided voters.
- Error is higher when the margin between the two candidates is lopsided.
- Error is higher the more days prior to Election Day the poll is conducted.

The Presidential Simulation

Silver predicts a lot of races: U.S. House, U.S. Senate and state governorships. The mother of all elections is, of course, the presidential.

If I were going to construct Silver's model for the Presidential election, I would set up 51 worksheets in

Excel. Each state worksheet would contain the polling data and weights for each state. We configure the 50 worksheets so each poll has its result, its weight, and its error. For one run of a simulation, each poll would have one value, producing one weighted average for the state. The winner would then be declared. Excel would assign the electoral votes for that state. The front worksheet of my Nate Silver model would show all 50 states, tally who gets more than 270 electoral votes, and predict the winner.

However, if you run the simulation, say, 10 million times, each poll has results that bounce around within its error, spitting out 10 million possible outcomes. When arrayed in a cumulative chart, all possible results are shown.

Understanding What Silver Says

One week before the 2012 Presidential election, Silver reported that President Obama had a 73 percent chance of being reelected. Of course, the prediction caused howls from Fox News, particularly from its loud, partisan, and woefully inaccurate bevy of taking heads. But while they bayed in protest, none explained exactly what Silver meant.

Silver ran his model eight days before the election. As I stated earlier, polls become more accurate closer to Election Day. Let's say that Silver ran his model 10 million times (with a new laptop this would take, oh, about four minutes). With states such as New York, California, Texas, or Georgia, the outcome was never in doubt. But in swing states such as Virginia, Florida, and particularly Ohio, the polls were too close to call. The winners may change for different iterations. If one runs the all possible iterations and combinations (and I would say that 10 million would probably cover it), then one can say how many times each side triumphs.

When Silver ran his models with the most current polls, 7.3 million times President Obama came out with more than 270 electoral votes; Mitt Romney won 2.7 million times. Thus, pronounced Silver, President Obama had a 73 percent chance of winning because he won 73 percent of the 10 million simulations.

Predicting the actual vote percentages is a little more difficult. However, when one had as much data as Silver, and the ability the run the simulations millions of times, the actual vote count will converge to the real number, much like crowdsourcing guesses often converge to the result.

Practical uses of Silver's model are abundant, and not solely on a presidential level. For example, if someone is working for a campaign in which the candidate is leading in the polls by 48 percent to 46 percent – a margin that is actually a statistical tie – a two months before Election Day, how likely is that candidate to actually win? And if he or she is behind by five points with one month to go, how much ground does the campaign really need to make up?

A prediction model can answer these questions. For example, if one candidate is leading by five points one month prior to Election Day in that or similar districts, 80 percent of the time he or she wins. This can be arrived at by looking at historical data. Or by plugging in all the current polls and financial data, and running the simulation 10 million times.

Why Models Like Silver's Always are More Accurate Than Pundits

Models like Nate Silver's consistently outperform pundits because they rely on data-driven analysis rather than subjective opinions or gut feelings. These models integrate vast amounts of data—polls, demographic trends, historical patterns—and apply rigorous statistical methods to identify probabilities and outcomes.

Unlike pundits, who often cherry-pick information to fit narratives, models remain impartial and grounded in evidence. They also adjust dynamically to new data, enhancing accuracy over time. Pundits, constrained by biases and sensationalism, rarely match the precision of models. In an era dominated by information overload, models offer a clearer, more reliable guide to understanding complex political landscapes.

Network Analysis and Political Strategy – Nordstrom? Center of Resistance?

Mathematical analysis provides valuable insights into current events. For instance, I conducted a Social Network Analysis Map of "@Nordstrom" serves as a great example.

The graph represents a network of 5,293 Twitter users whose recent tweets contained ""@Nordstrom"", or who were replied to or mentioned in those tweets, taken from a data set limited to a maximum of 5,000 tweets. The network was obtained from Twitter on Friday, 10 February 2017.

Figure 1 – Social Network Twitter Map "@Nordstrom"

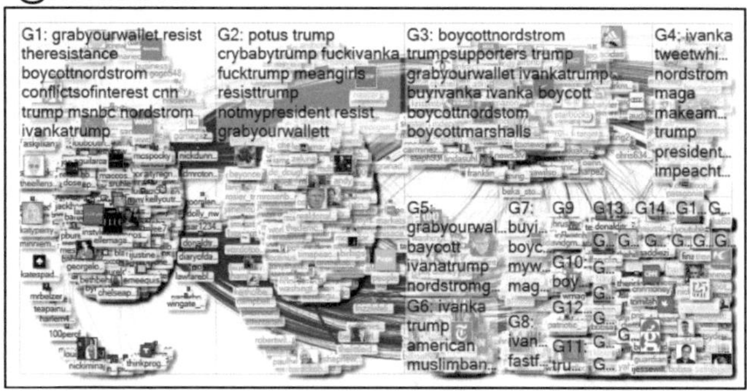

Social Network Analysis generates six main types of Twitter maps, one of which is known as a Polarized Network. This pattern appears when two groups are sharply divided in their views on a particular issue, resulting in two or more dense clusters with minimal interconnection. Polarized Twitter maps are often seen in discussions about highly contentious topics, such as women's rights in the Arab world or a fiercely contested gubernatorial race, for example, in Texas.

The most effective way to interpret the map is by examining how hashtags cluster within the software. In our analysis, three major groups emerge. Below is a breakdown of how the most dominant hashtags are clustered within these three largest groups.

Figure 2 – Top Hashtags - Social Network Twitter Map "@Nordstrom"

Top Hashtags in Tweet in G1:	Top Hashtags in Tweet in G2:	Top Hashtags in Tweet in G3:
[40] grabyourwallet	[10] potus	[102] boycottnordstrom
[34] resist	[7] trump	[46] trumpsupporters
[32] theresistance	[6] crybabytrump	[34] trump
[22] boycottnordstrom	[6] fuckivanka	[25] grabyourwallet
[22] conflictsofinterest	[6] fucktrump	[23] ivankatrump
[22] cnn	[5] meangirls	[20] buyivanka
[21] trump	[5] resisttrump	[17] ivanka
[21] msnbc	[4] notmypresident	[11] boycott
[20] nordstrom	[4] resist	[6] boycottnordstom
[13] ivankatrump	[4] grabyourwallett	[6] boycottmarshalls

It's clear that Group 1 (G1) consists of individuals who are mildly anti-Trump, likely including media figures and those dissatisfied with the new administration. Group 2 (G2) represents strong anti-Trump sentiment, while Group 3 (G3) appears to be supporters of the President and Ivanka's clothing line. The software captures every tweet in an Excel file, allowing for deeper analysis with text analytics if requested by the client.

The intriguing discovery is this: why has Nordstrom, a luxury department store chain typically located in upscale malls, become a symbol of resistance against the new administration? We believe we know the answer. What's fascinating is how clearly this emerges when we generate a Twitter map. Is the world turning upside down the new normal?

Social network visualization is now available online, helping to make sense of Big Data and presenting analysis results through emerging open-source programs. This type of analysis isn't limited to Twitter; it can also be applied to other social media platforms, large datasets, consumer sales data from major retailers like Walmart, or even survey data. It's an exciting new tool that, combined with our analytical expertise, enables us to deliver compelling insights to our clients.

A valuable application of this tool is tracking the impact of a major brand's new advertising campaign. By generating a Twitter network map daily over 30 days, we can measure the message's reach, identify which hashtags are going viral, observe how they cluster, and analyze the trending narrative over time.

Made in United States
Cleveland, OH
02 March 2025